Uncommon

An Essay on Pulp

D0584491

Uncommon

An Essay on Pulp

Owen Hatherley

Winchester, UK
Washington, USA

First published by Zero Books, 2011
Zero Books is an imprint of John Hunt Publishing Ltd., Laurel House, Station Approach,
Alresford, Hants, SO24 9JH, UK
office1@o-books.net
www.o-books.com

For distributor details and how to order please visit the 'Ordering' section on our website.

Text copyright: Owen Hatherley 2011

ISBN: 978 1 84694 877 0

A CIP catalogue record for this book is available from the British Library.

Design: Stuart Davies

Printed in the UK by CPI Antony Rowe
Printed in the USA by Offset Paperback Mfrs, Inc

We operate a distinctive and ethical publishing philosophy in all
areas of our business, from our global network of authors to
production and worldwide distribution.

CONTENTS

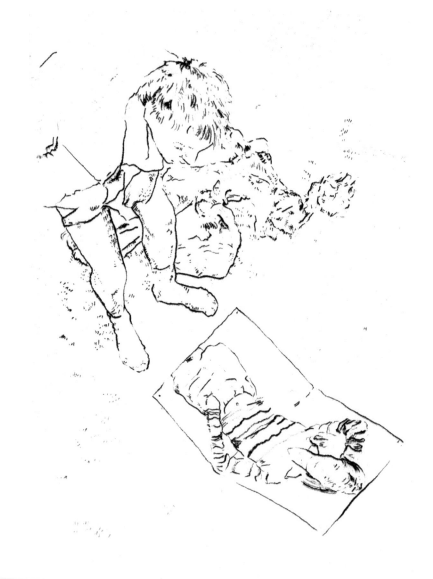

Intro

Apropos the transport shutdown due to the volcanic cloud there have been the inevitable outbreaks of Dunkirk spirit, with 'little ships' going out from the Channel ports to ferry home the stranded 'Brits'. It's a reminder of how irritating the Second War must have been, providing as it did almost unlimited opportunities for bossy individuals to cast themselves in would-be heroic roles while everyone else was just trying to get by. 'Brits'. So much of what is hateful about the world since Mrs Thatcher in that gritty little word.

Alan Bennett, Diaries, 19 April 2010

What if you never come down?

At the heart of this book is one of the most spectacular stories of emergence and disappearance in popular music - a group rising from the grimmest of circumstances to improbable success, followed by a decline of equal unlikeliness. Pulp formed in Sheffield in 1979, and released three sporadic, morbid, peculiar albums to zero commercial impact in 1983, 1987 and 1992. From 1994 they rose to sudden, unexpected prominence, and their singer became so well-known that he was invariably referred to by his first name. In 1995-6, they had several singles at number 2, an album at number 1, and an incident at an awards ceremony made them quite ridiculously famous. Then, when they returned in 1998, their singles failed to make the top 20, their albums received great reviews and sold in desultory amounts; their final gesture, a greatest hits album not entirely accurately titled *Hits*, barely even made the charts at all; when they split in 2002, it seemed hardly anyone had even remembered them. Many of their contemporaries lingered on, either making art-rock albums conspicuously without mockney accents, or purveying monobrowed pub rock to bafflingly enduring public affection. Jarvis Cocker endured as a National Treasure, although nobody seemed to quite remember what he was famous for - but Pulp had disappeared, leaving the world resolutely unchanged.

It is the argument of this book that Pulp were the last of a lineage, and that their rise and disappearance reflect the fate of that lineage. From the early 1970s onwards, a series of groups or individuals, from working or lower-middle class backgrounds, educated at art schools, claiming state benefits and living in bedsits or council flats months before they found themselves staying at five-star hotels, were thrown up in the UK. The Kinks, David Bowie, Roxy Music, Japan, Associates, Soft Cell, Kate Bush, The Fall, Pet Shop Boys, The Smiths, amongst others - all balanced some unstable combination of sexuality and literacy, ostentatious performance and austere rectitude, raging ambition and class resentment, translated into sonic documents balancing experimentation with populist cohesion; it was possible to read the lyric sheets without embarrassment, and for the most part you could dance, rather than flail or mosh, to it. At some point in the 1990s this literary-experimental pop tradition, completely inadequately subsumed under the rubric of 'indie', disappears, seemingly at its moment of greatest triumph. Some reasons for this are easily explained – workfare schemes meant that claiming the dole as a 'musicians' grant' was less and less practicable, council flats became unobtainable for any but the desperate, squats were all-but obliterated, while the contract between (a section of) the artistic intelligentsia and (a section of) the young working class that lay behind the art school was long since broken. The result was, and is, a striking homogeneity of class as much as of sound in British music. In a telling statistic, in October 2010, 60% of British artists in the UK top 10 had been to public school, compared with 1% in October 1990.

Pulp's status as the last of a line can be measured by the fact that, uniquely among the bands listed above, they have almost no successors. They had antecedents, of course, many of them listed above, but it's almost impossible to find bands explicitly citing them, let alone showing the effects of their musical example. If being generous, you can find some groups that fit the bill, but if so they're found at the margins - synthesiser primitives like Add N To X or Fat Truckers showed some hints of Pulp's sound and aesthetic, as did electro miserablists Ladytron; The All Seeing I's *Pickled Eggs and Sherbet* was thoroughly Pulpesque, but given that half of it was written by Jarvis Cocker, it could hardly not have been. Pulp's 1990-4 look and lyrical obsessions were plundered only by The Long Blondes, a Sheffield group who often seemed like an all-dancing, all-adultery, all-acrylic tribute to *His & Hers*. In the last couple of years, the post-Fordist laments of Mordant Music's *SyMptoMs* and Darkstar's *North* were signs the lineage hadn't completely vanished, owing little to Pulp but coming from similar psychological and geographical places - but neither were likely to dislodge the public schoolboys from the hearts of the youth. Especially when compared with the legions of imitators of contemporaries like Blur and Oasis, or even to the epigones of 2000s revivalists like Franz Ferdinand, Pulp left no legacy. At best, it is perhaps telling that the Arctic Monkeys, one of the only English groups to have (briefly) had any sort of zeitgeist-defining import in the last ten years, sang vignettes of South Yorkshire mundanity whose bleak cynicism and enlivening lechery often elicited Pulp comparisons, though neither their scally funk-rock nor their mildly self-deprecatory laddishness showed much affinity with their Sheffield forbears.

Yet when laments are made – and they often are – for this disappeared lineage, Pulp are seldom mentioned. In some right-thinking circles the mention of them elicits a roll of the eyes, and in others they receive a nostalgic adulation uncomfortably shared with all manner of 1990s culture criminals. In order to understand why Pulp are still either the object for unthinking scorn or *I Love the 90s* reminisce, their moment of populist fame is the likeliest culprit.

It needs to be said, and people are reluctant to say it - Pulp were not only by some measure the finest British group of the 1990s, but they compete with their more obvious forbears. Roxy Music, even at their most chillingly Helmut Newton-esque, never created as terrifying a vision of success and opulence achieved curdling into anomie and psychosis as 'This is Hardcore'; Morrissey never managed anything as perfectly vengeful as 'Common People', and the world created on their records from 1990-1994 is easily as obsessive, lyrically dense and inspired as The Fall at their peak. There's a critical consensus, largely administered by those who came of age in the 1970s or 80s, in which The Smiths, or maybe the final, purging whiteout of My Bloody Valentine, were *allowed* to be some sort of last gasp of the lineage outlined above, a consensus which wholly ignores the fact that in 1995 a group managed to send a krautrock epic about class warfare to number 2, and then used this public goodwill to convince tens of thousands to purchase a despairing six-minute dirge on the subject of amateur pornography three years later.

Some of the reasons for this critical timidity are entirely understandable - their undoubted collaboration with the horrible spectacle of Britpop, the notion that Pulp were dominated by their 'retro' signifiers, and most of all the ambiguous victory of Jarvis Cocker, pop celebrity. And as a lyricist, Cocker is complex and driven by some extremely recherché predilections, but is never abstract, always a realist of some sort, however particular or unforgiving that realism might be; unlike his idol and, eventually, producer Scott Walker, it's hard to imagine him switching from the kitchen sink to the elliptical, fragmented horrors of a *Tilt*. Nonetheless, this is a group that need to be taken seriously, very seriously indeed – and this book takes them as seriously as possible. The way into this is via the three things

4

which run through all their best work - class, sex and urbanism. But first, like fragments of alternatives lost in the grim torrent of historical inevitability, Pulp have to be rescued from the catastrophe that has befallen them.

If you want me, I'll be sleeping in throughout these glory days

Of all the confidence tricks and self-fulfilling prophecies that Britain has indulged in since 1979, the musical phenomenon known as Britpop must surely be one of the most spectacularly ill-conceived. Defined, according to taste or locale, by groups from the London Commuter Belt (estuary-accented would-be social anatomists like Blur, Menswear, Elastica, Echobelly, Sleeper) or South Lancashire (the vainglorious Manc/Scouse proleface tubthumping of Oasis, Cast, Northern Uproar), Britpop was a reductive, borderline racist distilling of English - seldom Scottish, Welsh or Irish - rock at its most rhythmically inert and vacantly optimistic, alongside a new line in Poujadist national resentment – officially at 'America', more implicitly against the mid-Atlantic, multiracial country the UK had become since the 1960s. Britpop brought to what was previously still perceptible as 'independent music' in both ethos and financial structure certain things it had long disdained. Sometimes, their rejections were hard to disagree with – at best Britpop had an upright, style-motivated rejection of the slovenly shuffling that marked many of their more righteously indie contemporaries, and it wisely broke with 'schmindie's smugly middle class disdain for the notion of the popular; but more often, Britpop threw several babies out with the bathwater. Suddenly, jingoism, proud idiocy and, most of all, giggly sexism became entirely acceptable again, and 'alternative' culture, from music to comedy to publishing, has never regained the basic human decencies that were quickly defined as 'humourless' and 'PC'. You can blame the New Lad culture which accompanied Britpop for the outright reactionary, middle-class-moron, 'men who should know better' world of *Nuts* magazine and Jimmy Carr (for an analysis of how this panned out in film, see Carl Neville's recent *Classless*).

In musical terms meanwhile, Britpop took the musical palette of 'indie' – already a hobbled, cramped reduction of the multi-valent independent music of the early 1980s into alternately inept or assured tributes to the Velvet Underground's third album – and made it even more relentlessly unimaginative, and even more ostrich-like with regard to the possibilities opened up by electronic and sampled musics. Britpop was a Mod Revival Revival, the mid-1990s' version of the late 1970s' version of the mid-1960s, with ever-diminishing returns. If this were all, or if Britpop coincided with a fallow period for non-guitar music, then it wouldn't be quite so offensive. This was far from the case.

At exactly the same time that Camden and Didsbury rocked with the sounds of Powder and Heavy Stereo, other musics were dominating the inner cities, and some of them even reached the attention of the music press. There was the 'lost generation' of experimental groups like Disco Inferno, Bark Psychosis and Seefeel, for which the term Post-Rock was first coined; but they disappeared without trace. Contrition is sometimes offered for Britpop's ignorance of what was called, in a neologism almost as ugly as Britpop itself, Trip-Hop, which consisted of three excellent acts from Bristol and legions of imitators as poor as the second-rank Britpoppers. The *NME*'s critics, in their erstwhile role as indie's conscience, quite rightly made Tricky's *Maxinquaye* rather than *The Great Escape* or *(What's the Story) Morning Glory?* their album of 1995. Yet, and much more dubiously, Britpop, in its 1994-7 reign, also coincided with and obscured the explosive, multiracial, working class rhythmic psychedelia of Jungle, unarguably the most original and futuristic music ever made in these islands. At the time, the junglist's disgust with these ridiculous retro fantasies was expressed best when Simon

Reynolds devoted the singles column in *Melody Maker* solely to Jungle 12"s, while his colleagues were hailing Smaller or Plastic Fantastic; elsewhere, Mark Fisher in the *New Statesman* pointed out that the mid-60s' modernism, with its culture of newness, dance music and sharp dressing, was continued by fans of Metalheadz and Suburban Base more than the followers of Ocean Colour Scene. It's understandably hard now to convince anyone who spent their weekends at raves rather than watching *TFI Friday* that anything produced by Britpop had any merit. Yet, when the Blur-Oasis chart battle made the 6 o'clock News it was obvious that resistance was futile.

Alan Bennett recently wrote, accurately, that many of the worst things about the last thirty years are all encapsulated in the mere word, *Brit*. It's a word that immediately suggests lumpen jingoism, flag-waving, backwardness, imperial revanchism, general thuggery - so it's appropriate that its only use in a pop music context was so egregious. Yet at the time, for some – and having turned 14 in 1995, I can fully attest to this – things felt very different. Aside from a suppressed sonic amazement, myself and my friends at a south coast comprehensive had little interest in Jungle; like Happy Hardcore, it was the music the kids that beat us up listened to (although in a nice irony, by 2004 practically all of us were compulsively listening to the music from 1994 that we certainly weren't listening to at the time). What *did* appeal was Britpop, not so much because of a liking for the Union Jack, sugary tea or re-runs of *Quadrophenia*, but because it seemed to be music made by 'us' – by bullied kids who were good at school, but who had somehow propelled themselves onto the radio and the television. We weren't particularly discerning – few teenagers are – so we eagerly soaked up the entire lot, going to see *everyone* play, from Marion to the Longpigs to Bis. The sense that 'we' had taken over was strengthened on the rare occasions when something or someone genuinely other made the charts, as when David McAlmont briefly became a star with the grandiloquent 'Yes', when Jyoti Mishra's White Town got a freak number 1 with the poignantly tortured bedroom melodrama of 'Your Woman', and most of all through awkward, skinny, bespectacled working-class intellectual Jarvis Cocker's moment of celebrity.

There's no doubt that Pulp were absolutely intrinsic to Britpop in all of its aspects; at times, they might have been its figureheads. I vividly remember them stealing the show in the 1995 television special *Britpop Now!*, a showcase for various English guitar-brandishers presented for the first time as a coherent and named movement. It felt incredibly exciting, a moment of victory. Yet now it's subsumed in the memory as fully part of the manifold horrors that defined the mid-late 1990s: the omnipresent 'mindless Northern bluff' (as Luke Haines put it) of Oasis, the election of a Thatcherite lawyer as Labour Prime Minister, the 1996 European Championship and the appalling 'Three Lions', the British public's sudden, queasily surreal reversion to a penitent peasantry in response to the death of Diana Spencer.

There is a persistent temptation to compare Britpop very closely to New Labour, an analogy convincingly made in John Harris' politically astute, if musically unrepentant tome *The Last Party – Britpop, Blair and the Demise of British Rock*. In both cases – the coup in the pop charts in 1995-6, the election in May 1997 - it seemed like 'our' side had won, but it soon became clear that, in its pursuit of success at any cost, it had internalised every single one of its opponents' values, all taken to heart with the indiscriminate zeal of the recent convert. The common factor linking Blair and Blur is that they made thoroughly sure to *get their sell-out in first*, to make perfectly clear that the dream was over, that there would be no more experiments, no more utopias, only a constricted, and as the still-unfolding financial crisis makes clear, utterly misnamed 'realism'. The generation that came of age in the mid-late 1990s were perhaps the most apolitical of the 20th century, leaving a mess which those born in that decade are struggling to clear up, through the student movement against the Tory-Whig Coalition government – whose Prime Minister, a fan of the Smiths and the Jam, displays impeccably Britpop tastes. Pulp were alone at the time in holding onto the possibility of utopias and alternatives, in being able to use the word 'socialism' without smirking – although they didn't create an alternative so much as carry the idea through a most unsympathetic period.

But recently, it seems like there isn't even a need for an apologia. Britpop has been surprisingly fondly remembered, at least in some circles. *The Last Party* and an accompanying documentary gave it an ennobling historical treatment, making a tactical acknowledgement of the awfulness of most of the music in order to make improbable claims for the 'avant-garde' nature of Suede, Elastica and Blur. Harris constantly laments Britpop's lack of sonic imagination, but is equally disdainful when a group steps outside of the format of spiky 7" singles, into the 'pretension' of Suede's *Dog Man Star* or Pulp's 'dated' *His 'N' Hers*, both of which showed a conspicuous and unforgivable lack of quirky guitar choons. Following Harris' book was a rash of memoirs, from Britpop apostate Luke Haines' *Bad Vibes* to Britpop queen turned chick-lit novelist Louise Wener's *Different for Girls*, reinforcing the notion that this was truly A Significant Moment. Everyone has reformed, from Suede and Blur at the top, all the way down to Kula Shaker and Shed Seven at the bottom, to play a nostalgia-for-nostalgia circuit. Horrifyingly, the mid-2000s saw the success of several Britpop revivalist groups such as The Libertines and Kaiser Chiefs. Like the original Britpop, this movement was a depressingly successful reaction against modernity – in the early 2000s, the *NME* made a swerve into coverage of electronic music, R&B and hip hop, but covers for Aphex Twin, Godspeed You! Black Emperor, Destiny's Child and Missy Elliott did not go down well with the readers; as is known, the *NME*'s circulation has always plummeted when a black artist is on the cover. A hastily cobbled-together 'New Rock Revolution' quickly replaced this experiment in pop-cultural *Glasnost*, soon vindicated by the commercial success of such as Franz Ferdinand. In the process, an already stagnant gene pool was reduced to positively Romanov levels.

Is this the way the future's meant to feel?

In one of the few serious books about the pop culture of the 1990s, Michael Bracewell's *The Nineties – When Surface Was Depth*, the inability of anyone who had been raised on the lineage of literate, experimental English pop to see much worth in Britpop is unsurprisingly clear; yet so is an inability to notice when that lineage is being continued rather than simulated. Bracewell's brief treatment of Britpop, which he rightly regards as an 'infantilist nostalgia', accuses Pulp, rather bizarrely, of 'impersonating The Kinks' but manfully concedes that 'I Want To Live Like Common People' (sic) might have been a 'glorious pop moment' comparable to the title track of Oasis' *What's the Story*. Suede, whose well-rehearsed sexual ambiguity and extensive reading of *England's Dreaming* meant they already spoke Bracewell's language, receive much more sympathy, despite being a far more unambiguously 'retro' group than Pulp. The only other mention of Pulp is later on in *When Surface Was Depth*, where, in a chapter on the '90s phenomenon of 'Retro', Bryan Ferry states his appreciation of (titled correctly this time) 'Common People'. The rest of the chapter is devoted to Roxy Music, advancing the theory that 1970s pop culture was based on 'the shock of the old as a presentiment of the future', an 'indigenous time-travel' and 'chronological dandyism' of which Roxy Music were the pre-eminent example. For Bracewell, by the time of Pulp or Suede this has degenerated into a fetish for 'the landscape of an English adolescence in the 1970s' – the law of diminishing returns, again, with the nostalgia suddenly obvious, based on actual childhood memory, with the spell now broken.

What Bracewell didn't notice, and it is hardly surprising given the book's prevailing air of seen-it-all boomerism, was both just how true this was, and how in Pulp's case this actually opens up something much more interesting than the mere revivalism that he thinks he's hearing. For Pulp, the imaginary 1970s were a *portal*, a transforming force, not a real remembered thing. Pulp were the first major carriers in Pop of what has since been called Nostalgia for the Future, a Futurism that is dated to the 1970s as the last time that viable political, urban and stylistic alternatives really existed; and which has since been codified as 'Hauntology', via a landscape of BBC Radiophonic Workshop, Pelican Books, public information films and Municipal Modernism bent awry through the gaps and aporias of memory, with half-remembered horror films shaking the stiltedness of BBC English into uncanny incantations. Almost all of the above were present and correct in Pulp's work, but the persistent sexual and personal urgency of their music – not to mention the lack of 'ghostly' signifiers – sets them apart from its snugly contemplative warmth. If much hauntological music can sound like a means of filling the time while we wait for the future to start up again, then Pulp's persistent desperation, their sense of time running out, demands that the future-past resume itself immediately.

Pulp's 1970s references are absolutely undeniable, of course, and they can be easily listed – the (in both senses) fetish for luridly coloured artificial fabrics, for pop-modernist design, for antiquated analogue synthesisers, and for the cities remade by post-war 'comprehensive redevelopment', alongside an eroticism informed more by Chris Foss' soft-focus illustrations to Dr Alex Comfort's *The Joy of Sex* than by the hard, active bodies of 1980s-90s R&B. This isn't so much a nostalgia for a real, lost past or for a carefree childhood, as you might find respectively in

Blur and Supergrass, but nostalgia for something that *didn't* happen, for cities that were never really built, for musical instruments which never became the norm, for sex which was never supposed to be about health and efficiency. In this, Pulp's 1970s is easily as charged as Roxy Music's 1930s. It's unclear why it is that Al Bowlly and interwar tailoring are acceptable pop-cultural influences while Frank Farian and Bri-Nylon are not, but the reason might be that it's all too close to Bracewell – it takes someone who doesn't actually remember the 1970s to be able to find some potential in it.

It is no coincidence whatsoever that Pulp were from Sheffield, the provincial city that, perhaps more than any other in the UK, attempted to create a viable modernist landscape between the 1950s and 1970s, before the money ran out when the steel industry restructured itself and sacked most of its workforce, and a council attempting 'Socialism in One City' were squeezed of any funds. Its wildly overambitious Brutalist buildings, left in ruins or demolished altogether in the 1990s, provided – still provide - a landscape where there's space to dream of what could have been, and to move from there to thinking of what could still be. From their earliest records in the early '80s to the early 2000s, there's a persistent, direct and occasionally too-close-to-the-bone attention to male-female relations in Pulp's work, but it's when they leave this town at the end of the decade – and return there, to write about it, suddenly seeing it anew – that their work transforms, that they become a band worth writing tortuous monographs about. From *Separations* (recorded mostly in 1989) to 2001's 'Wickerman', Pulp excelled at the evocation of a devastated but still very much alive post-industrial city, and the lives, loves and explorations that go on inside it. It's arguable that their determined urbanism – as opposed to Britpop's suburbanism – was informed by having been told, throughout their 1970s childhoods, that their city would be the site of the future, something that is far harder to believe if you grew up in the 1980s or 1990s.

Alongside that is the collectivity of the city itself; as often as the protagonist of a Pulp song is a voyeur, he or she is also entirely *of* the crowd.

If it's the conjunction of sex and the city that infuses Pulp's finest moments, then their attention to the former is also worth wresting away from both 1990s lad culture and 1970s glamour. Jarvis Cocker, almost uniquely among male Pop lyricists, was and is a great writer of female characters, which mixes sometimes uncomfortably with songs of sex-as-class-revenge. In Bracewell's beloved Roxy Music, women are untouchable, airbrushed and pneumatic pin-up girls or nameless, unknowable objects of quasi-Lacanian, impossible-to-fulfil desire. In neither case do they have perceptible thoughts, let alone desires; they're objects, and this point is so obvious that it isn't intended as a critique, merely an observation of an important and overlooked difference. It's interesting that it's this which is considered an example of *sui generis* Pop Art, while the complicated, human female protagonists of so many Pulp songs are merely an instance of Kinks imitation. In this, most groups who have made a fetish of their sexual ambiguity are alike – from 'Suffragette City' to 'Animal Nitrate', women are there to either a) shag or b) to lament over when they will no longer shag you. Aside from, but undeniably inextricably linked with, Pulp's unusually reconstructed attention to matters of gender, is their preoccupation with sex. Britpop, as Bracewell rightly notes when he draws attention to its childishness, was mostly as terrified by sex as it was terrified by modernity, for all its leering laddism (though the somewhat more *adult* Elastica and Suede records are obvious exceptions here). Pulp's articulation of sexual obsession, sexual anticipation, sex as instrument in the class war and finally sexual disgust, is absolutely unique in pop. If really groping for analogies, you could compare some of it to Prince, were he ever capable of admitting to inadequacy or doubt. If this conjunction of sexuality and space runs through their work and this book, there's another aspect that cannot be overlooked.

So imagine there's a film, and you're the star

Pulp were the last major group to both be consciously working class and to be consciously, unashamedly arty; the last to be notably proud of being northern and proletarian while remaining quite unabashed about their intelligence. In fact, an inquisitive class-credentials Commissar would find their singer's rep somewhat tarnished by the fact that his mother once stood for election as a Conservative councillor, but would also be entirely satisfied by the stories of stoic poverty you can find in any biography of the group and its members. Like their attention to Sheffield's singular qualities, their class-consciousness was also formed by leaving the city – Jarvis Cocker has said that he didn't feel working class until he went to St Martin's College in the late 1980s, encountering the real middle class and its very real privileges. Either way, in a decade where John Major claimed he was creating a 'classless society' and Tony Blair and John Prescott pronounced that we were all middle class now, Pulp's persistent sense of resentment, historical injustice and their revelling in partial, tit-for-tat revenge was extremely conspicuous, shared only at the time (and in a more musically leaden manner) by the Manic Street Preachers. In *Different Class*, they soundtracked the abolition of Clause 4 with a what was effectively a concept album about the persistence of class warfare.

There's a contradiction at the heart of this. What Pulp had in common most of all with the lineage outlined at the start of this introduction was a certain *vengeful self-creation;* the sense that they, like Bowie, Bryan Ferry, Siouxsie Sioux, David Sylvian, Morrissey, Richey Edwards or countless legions of bored suburban stars who never made it into the spotlight, had spent their lives transforming themselves into characters, with countless hours in their terrace, semi or tower-block bedrooms devoted to achieving the exact conjunction that would make them unique, and that they could then use as a weapon against a world that had already wronged them beyond forgiveness. Usually, this involves deliberately exacerbating what are seen as flaws in the outside world; overemphasising to the point of either absurdity or charisma particular defects of figure, appearance and manner, whether an effeminate flounce or a doleful murmur. With some, this phase of creation lasted a couple of years, meaning that once they had achieved that perfect look, that impregnable aesthetic, it was fixed forever, and they were doomed to the perpetual, if lucrative, self-parody that Morrissey or Ferry's careers devolved into. Pulp avoided that fate largely because that phase had lasted so long for them – over a decade, in their case, of considering yourself a star while the rest of the world considers you scum. It meant also that when they had their moment, in the fifteen minutes they had allotted, they were especially gleeful in their revenge.

This isn't the same as the more straightforward grafting narrative of working hard until you become a competent sportsman or a rock journeyman. The use of this particularly American escape route hasn't disappeared quite without trace, and can be found as an abundant motif in the lyrics of grime and gangsta, along with an attendant 'Aim High!' managerial conformism, albeit one that still provides explosions of momentary joy, like the thrill of Dizzee Rascal's awkward, geeky whine cutting into the dulcet Bullingdon tones of most contemporary rock singers. The point remains, though, that this escape route is also a route to conformism and acceptance, to the Thatcherite bargain that You Can Do It. The problem with this is also the problem with the vengeful self-creation – by definition, it is never collective. In fact, it's always based on the yearning to get *out* of a stifling working-class environment, with the concomitant knowledge that your ability, your looks, or your ego mark you out, something which was once a curse and is now a blessing. *You* might get out, but most are still stuck here.

This is where the genuinely transformative part of Pulp's work comes in. In an essay in 1917 called 'Art as Device', the Russian Formalist Viktor Shklovsky wrote of how the best novels use something he called *Ostranienie*, 'making strange' or 'estrangement', a technique that makes the most mundane daily acts into extraordinary rituals, inducing like a revelation the feeling that, in fact, these things which purported to be entirely normal, entirely regular and entirely unremarkable were in fact deeply odd, extremely 'unnatural'. In so doing, they enable the reader to see the world anew. It is the device of *Ostranienie* that Pulp used on their finest records - and it's this that really made them significant. Whether it's the post-industrial adventures of 'My Legendary Girlfriend', the South Yorks travelogues of 'Sheffield: Sex City' or 'Inside Susan', the prurient anthropology of *His & Hers*, the marriage-told-through-objects of 'Live Bed Show', the pornographic horror of 'This is Hardcore' or the late, melancholic rural retreat of 'The Trees', Pulp's records are invariably 'about' things which could be related in a markedly tedious fashion, were the narrator so inclined. Instead, home furnishings, cul-de-sacs and council estates become the matter of the utmost carnal melodrama.

Pulp did this most impressively on *His & Hers*, *Separations*, the singles collected on *Intro*, the thrilling perversions of *Sisters* - here, they were not *commenting* on things, as were the above-it-all aspiring satirists of Britpop; instead, they were constructing a world, piecing something together, creating out of forgotten ephemera and hated remnants a new mode of seeing. The place they created bore a great deal of relation to the Britain of the 1990s, particularly the urban and inner-suburban environments of a pre-regeneration era. But rather than reproducing it as kitchen sink realism, these places were instead refracted and transfigured, made extraordinary, albeit without any of the magic-realist kitsch that might imply. Mercifully, nobody actually physically transforms, never ascends to heaven or owt like that in a Pulp record. Throughout, the everyday was never glumly accepted, as it is in, say, the records of the Arctic Monkeys; but skewed, revealed in its full strangeness. You could find here a way of looking at the environment around you, and your relation to it, that just wasn't otherwise available in novel, film or, least of all, pop record.

The particularly extreme environment of Sheffield might have been completely intrinsic to the forming of this sound, but not to its reception. I didn't even *visit* Sheffield until over a decade later, but instead found analogies for Stanhope Road, Lyndhurst Grove, Park Hill, Pitsmoor, in the districts, streets and estates of a blitzed south coast port, like Sheffield the sort of post-industrial town written off as a collection of concrete eyesores by the discerning traveller. Importantly, this exploration of suddenly unfamiliar space wasn't a solitary matter, not a *bloke* thing – it was an obsession which I and another embarked on together; and when we started doing so, 'Do You Remember the First Time' was anticipatory, not retrospective. It warned us it might be disappointing. When Pulp sang of collective orgasms in Sheffield tower blocks, we had no idea what Park Hill looked like (certainly not that it had been listed by English Heritage), but related it to a rather less architecturally remarkable 20-storey slab that loomed over the terraces where we lived. The net-curtain twitching that runs through these records sustained us through walks around endless streets of semis, making them appear as dens of secrets and intrigue; and the group's fetish for the second-hand, for picking improbable gems out of the jumble, resonated particularly well in a place where the High Street had nine charity shops.

Although these songs animated our alternate impatient frustration and morbid, compulsive fascination with the depressed cities where we lived, they also oriented us outwards, into an obsession with London as escape. Legions of trapped provincials identified with 'Countdown', where Cocker swears his eventual departure from his hometown, shared that desperation and anticipation - and followed suit, following all the prescriptions to the letter, and it's never a great idea to base your life on the prescriptions of pop music. There's little doubt these songs made us overly self-involved – 'so imagine there's a film, and you're the star', and we did – but the same thing happened to thousands of others, and that original egotism maybe, tentatively, became something collective, a fierce identification with difference and place, particularly places which had become denigrated and dilapidated. And the movement need not be centrifugal – some of the southerners among us relocated from London to Sheffield in order to discover this 'Sex City' at first hand, perhaps finding what they were looking for, more likely running into something else entirely.

If there is anything of value to the – ahem – 'Brit' centric nature of this pop music, it isn't because it said something eternal and comforting about the English character, not because it instilled a vague feeling of togetherness or an aloof sense of social superiority. Instead, it's in the way that these records transformed the towers, terraces, malls and streets around, or rather the way they revealed something in them that we could never possibly have noticed otherwise. They whispered that the apparently drab and miserable towns of the British Isles were replete with layers of interest and intrigue, more than any other, if you peered into them closely enough. Take your year in Provence - shove it up your arse.

You're gonna like it – but not a lot

What this book isn't, as may already be clear, is a biography of Pulp, or of Jarvis Cocker. I'll take this opportunity to direct anyone looking for such a thing to Mark Sturdy's admirable and comprehensive *Pulp – Truth and Beauty*, as their story in biographical terms is an extraordinary one, and it is not recapitulated here.

What this book is, is an extended essay on the group's records themselves, taking the line that the artist's actual intentions are secondary, and that once they have let a work out into the world, they've lost control over it. It takes the view that lyrics are worthy of investigation and analysis. This has not been a popular approach in pop criticism for some time, seen too often as simple point-missing – as Phil Spector once told Tom Wolfe when the lyrics to his hits were criticised for being infantile and asinine, they don't mention the beat. The history of Dylanology, or the analysis of what is primarily a music for dancing and listening to as if it was English Lit, has given such analyses a bad name. However, one way of measuring a group's importance – especially in the lineage outlined above – is how their lyrics, as much as their sleeves and their aesthetic, manage to connect to an audience, how they manage to put into words what it is thinking, or to make you think things you've never thought before. Currently, the Spector view of lyrics' insignificance is entirely dominant, and it accompanies a strikingly bleak Tin Pan Alley resurgence across Reality TV pop, one denuded of wit, sex, drama, class, politics. Even in 'alternative' music, the reason why quite good, eminently danceable or sonically imaginative groups from The Rapture to Animal Collective seemed so unimpressive compared to their inspirations is because they have, literally, *nothing to say* – they communicate nothing, they aren't much interested in communicating much more than their own blankness and grooviness. That's marvellous if you like that sort of thing, but the notion that it subverts some sort of logocentric rockism is conformism masquerading as critique. Pulp had something to say, and this is not insignificant.

This book is, then, a series of investigations into Pulp's 20 years or so of music, a book about pop aesthetics, an argument about pop's continued or erstwhile importance, and it is advocacy for Pulp's ability to answer, in some very unexpected ways, questions of urbanism, sexuality and class. It is unashamedly subjective and driven – as again is probably clear – by fandom, although it will be critical of the group's occasional major lapses. If you want to know the actual story, read Mark Sturdy; and for a wider account of Britpop and its political dabblings, along with the key questions of who was shagging who, who was taking smack and who was not, John Harris' *The Last Party* is invaluable.

And as we're dealing here with a created world, and an intensely visual one, each chapter begins with an etching by Lisa Cradduck.

I feel obliged, given the extensive quotations from lyrics, to ask: please do not read the words whilst listening to the recordings.

I

Of Freaks and Men

Maybe this gets down to it: the Ronettes, the Shangri-Las, the Crystals, the guy singers too, all those old classic rock & roll songs, were fuelled by one thing: sexual repression, and consequent frustration. They may have been sexist, they may have been neurotic or masochistic – sometimes I think the whole reason pop music was invented in the first place was to vent sick emotions in a deceptively lulling form. They were literally explosive with all that pent-up lust and fear and guilt and dread and hate and resentment and confusion.
Lester Bangs, *Blondie* (1980)

Some people laugh at my lighthouse

Let's start at the beginning, which in Pulp's case is a very far back indeed. They formed as Arabacus Pulp at a Sheffield comprehensive in 1978, with Jarvis Cocker being the only member who would remain in the group by 1984. Their first recordings date from three years later, - a John Peel Session broadcast in 1981, which the band blocked from release for years, eventually relenting after Peel's death. The recordings show a quintessential minor post-punk group, a typical 'John Peel band' of the era. In fact, with this and their subsequent first album *It*, a case could be made that Pulp were the sort of band about which Pulp themselves would later have been nostalgic – a perfect example of a period's minor literature, and fascinating for its insight into a prelapsarian moment before all the guilt and the anger and the lust came in.

The four songs on the Peel Session showcase a group trying

out various fashionable modes, most sounding very accomplished, with all manner of fancy instrumental touches backing surprisingly confident, if audibly very youthful crooning. 'Please Don't Worry' is a bouncy, grinningly cheerful song which sounds like a minor Britpop single from 15 years later, its proto-indie galumphing marked out only by the first stirrings of what would later be a waspish sarcasm ('think of all the money that's gone to your waist' croons our callow singer). 'Refuse to be Blind' is rote post-punk, evoking the Comsat Angels without the drama; but the other two tracks suggest that even this early on, there was something here other than enthusiasm and studied borrowings. The unfortunately titled 'Turkey Mambo Momma' is saturated in the clattering punk-funk of the Pop Group and its outgrowths like Pigbag, nervous, gawky and with a clumsy, disjointed rhythmic compulsion; the yelping vocal sounds more like the Jarvis of the 1990s than the ill-advised croon he would adopt for the rest of the '80s. 'Wishful Thinking' is a love song to the idea of being in love, written by someone who clearly hadn't been, a rather beautiful, winsome, heartfelt and slightly ridiculous serenade, with only a Peter Hook bassline pulling it out of easy listening territory.

Which is precisely where Pulp are headed next, with their first album in 1983, the punning *It*, recorded for Cherry Red, and very much of a piece with their presciently retro roster – Everything But The Girl or the Marine Girls are an apposite comparison. Most of the songs follow on from 'Wishful Thinking's naïve balladry. That song is included here, with any hints of post-punk stripped away, replaced by an expensive-sounding production full of woodwinds, reverb, female backing vocals and warm acoustic guitars, placed in some vague, gauzy late 1960s-cum-early-80s, evoking the likes of Lee Hazelwood or Bobbie Gentry, only with vocals by a South Yorkshire schoolboy. In both sound and subject matter, *It* resembles the first couple of Leonard Cohen albums without the experience, or most obviously the sex.

Accordingly, the record is as shallow as it is pretty, although it's not without an alternately lush and gawky charm. When re-released in the mid-90s to cash in on 'Common People', one music press reviewer marvelled at how, on this evidence, Gregory from *Gregory's Girl* had morphed over a decade into Johnny from *Naked*. The songs' sheer youthfulness often tips over into an admittedly quite delightful bathos - the extended metaphor of 'My Lighthouse' is the silliest moment, where Jarvis asks a woman to visit his 'high tower' without, from the sound of it, any sense that this might elicit the odd *fnarr*. But rather than being completely out of kilter with their later work, *It* is a preview of what Pulp would often become at their least inspired; 'classic' acoustic homilies like 'Something Changed' or 'Birds in Your Garden' could easily have fit on it, and the songs' tendency to be somewhat leaden and classicist suggests, like some of Cocker's solo albums, what happens when the singer is left on his own.

At another pole from all this conservatism is the loveliest of *It*'s diversions, the dreamlike 'Blue Girls', where our protagonist watches sunbathing women at a seaside resort, to a beatless melange of flutes and echoing voices. It has a haunting stillness, a perfect, undisturbed happiness unencumbered by any of the angst or responsibility of adulthood (or indeed of puberty) – it evokes, as much as does *Gregory's Girl*, a sun-dappled 1970s, with Cumbernauld replaced by Sheffield's *jolie-laide* hillscape. However, there's a very embryonic eye here too, an observation of flaking skin, ageing bodies, the passing of time, all just out of shot. 'There Was', a b-side from the same time, has a similar elegant, wistful melancholy, but after the failure of its a-side, an attempt to 'make a single like Wham!' called 'Everybody's Problem', the group that recorded *It* collapses. Around the same time, as detailed in Pulp's own 1994 documentary film *Do you remember the first time?*, Jarvis Cocker loses his virginity, and the group change very quickly indeed into an altogether more murky proposition.

A hole in your heart, and one between your legs

Irrespective of her politics, Cocker's mum was a single parent in an unglamorous part of South Yorkshire, who by all accounts formerly harboured artistic aspirations before having to shelve them to bring up children alone. She is, according to the group's own account, the subject matter of the 1985 single 'Little Girl (with Blue Eyes)'. This was released on Fire records, with whom the group would reluctantly remain until 1992, and marks the first time that Pulp actually sound like *Pulp* – not surprisingly, as it's at this point that keyboard player Candida Doyle and violinist-guitarist-conceptualist Russell Senior join the group. What was taken at the time to be a naughtily Nabokovian title is merely the description of a young woman charmed into marriage and childbirth, cheated into domesticity and cheated of her hopes for something more - 'so just forget about your paintings, cause you've got to get the washing done'. The arrangement is not a million miles from the late 60s MOR of *It*, except here the chorus' tip into melodrama creates unease rather than a comforting warmth. What makes 'Little Girl' especially interesting is the delivery – the undercurrent of triumph and taunting. With respect to the girl with 'a hole in your heart, and one between your legs...you've never had to wonder which one he's going to fill' you wonder, not for the first time, whether the song's protagonist is an observer of the woman's plight or a participant; while the song is deeply sympathetic, there's not much doubt that the man in it is fully implicated.

'Little Girl' was followed by the rather less impressive 'Dogs are Everywhere', another extended metaphor set to clumsily played uneasy listening, this time for the slavering, canine resemblances of the Sheffield male; like 'Little Girl', though, the group held it in enough affection to play it live as late as 1995. The other songs from this particularly commercially unsuccessful time – collected on the compilation *Masters of the Universe* in 1994 - show a sudden attention to sex, a sudden *fixation*, and its view on matters carnal is not optimistic. Pulp were, unintentionally or otherwise, echoing the similarly anguished postures of a group from the other side of the Pennines – they could also have sung a line like 'god, how sex implores you...to let yourself lose yourself...', but they weren't capable at this stage of putting their angst into anything as seductively uncertain as 'Stretch out and Wait' or to as proudly inept as 'Handsome Devil'. Pulp were apt to disassociate themselves from The Smiths in interviews, which seems a matter of the narcissism of small differences as much as a sense of inferiority and jealousy. This one-sided rivalry extended as far as the Pulp aesthetic, quite unintentionally. After a fall from a third-floor window – apparently to impress a girl – Jarvis Cocker was confined to a wheelchair for some time. Photographs of Pulp concerts from the mid-1980s show a worryingly thin frontman with a straggly goatee on his lantern jaw, with the whole bag of bones bundled into an ill-fitting suit, with an aggrieved sneer on his face, making hand gestures in his chair. Reviewers at the time thought it an attempt to emulate Morrissey and his hearing aid. Looking at images of this unfortunate figure, especially when compared with the deeply handsome Smiths frontman, these songs' declaration of total exclusion seems even more clearclearer. You could imagine a simmering feeling towards the Mancunian of 'call *yourself* an outcast, with your James Dean looks and your bared chest?' Pulp in 1986 really were sick, dull and plain.

Nonetheless, as is obvious from the songs later assembled on *Masters of the Universe*, the two groups were united in their sceptical view of copulation and the enjoyability thereof. In 'Mark of the Devil', for instance, sex is straightforwardly torture; the record's post-punk polka suggests the Slavophile influence of Russell Senior, as does the revelling in masochism – the martial beat suddenly stops dead to usher in a crooned plaint that 'your past is just a bedroom full of implements of cruelty'. A 1985 TV show on 'Sheffield Bands' (lamenting their disappearance from the public eye after The Human League and Cabaret Voltaire) features the group playing the song surrounded by unfolded loo roll; Senior, standing bolt upright and staring intensely, looks much more of a star than an emaciated, desperately uncomfortable-looking Cocker. They appear in an interview section, discussing, with heavy sarcasm, the overlooked beauty of Sheffield and lamenting how student venues 'act like they're doing you a favour' if they deign to offer you a gig; and with particular bitterness, note how in Sheffield musicians are not terribly respected, 'because you're all scum on social security'. The film gives the impression of a deeply unhappy time and place, while the camera loops round and round Park Hill, this time in its obvious meaning as Urban Blight. And given what was happening then in the city that housed the NUM's headquarters – and the subject matter of Pulp's last recorded song, 'The Last Day of the Miners' Strike' – you might expect some hint of politics to their palpable resentment and anger, especially given that Russell Senior was a flying picket at the time. Yet as he recalled in a 2009 interview, Cocker felt little solidarity with miners who were otherwise the lads that beat him up every weekend.

Accordingly, the hatreds and dramas stay at a resolutely personal level, remaining in uncomfortable bedrooms, icy bedsits, with any conflicts being those between two people. The universalisation of all that resentment comes much later. For all that, some of these songs are becoming rich with observation, showing a lyricist starting to sharpen. Most of all, they display an attention to minutiae – from facial expressions to furnishings - that is increasingly striking; '97 Lovers', where a farfisa drone lies beneath the crooned tale of a woman who joylessly sleeps with a builder beneath a poster of Roger Moore, is the first sign of the eye that would write *His 'N' Hers*. In the cinematic 'Blue Glow', meanwhile, anticipation, or fear, builds towards a midnight encounter. Pulp also were audibly going towards something, but, if we regard their series of false starts, mistakes and disasters as a teleological advance towards the group they would become, we have first a detour into an aesthetic of relentless morbidity.

I'll keep you and I'll throw myself away

The bleakness becomes particularly unpalatable on *Freaks*, surely one of the most lugubrious albums ever recorded. Without ever being a particularly good record, *Freaks* is at least worthy of its own chapter in Simon Reynolds and Joy Press' Freudian pop history *The Sex Revolts*, documenting as it does with unusual pungency and honestly a certain fear of coupling which runs through decades of pop. *Freaks* is much better encompassed by its prolix subtitle *Ten Stories About Power, Claustrophobia, Suffocation and Holding Hands,* rather than its obvious rubric, as it's not so much the study of difference and general noncon-formist freakishness that one might expect, either from the title or from Pulp's later work. Apart from Russell Senior's two songs here, 'Fairground' and 'Anorexic Beauty', both of which cleave to the programme in their staccato, third-person manner, and the small-town terror of 'Being Followed Home', *Freaks* is an album about an interminable relationship – indeed, the one moment where it tries to shake itself out of its inertia, the Mitteleuropean flail of 'The Never-Ending Story', sounds like a purging attempt to finish some sort of real-life (un)romantic horror of a relationship. Accordingly, there is a lot of sex on *Freaks*, but it's very bad sex indeed. Outside of the warring couple, we've got some vignettes about masturbation, megalomania and anorexia. 'Disco 2000' this is not.

Sadly, given that it's entirely possible to channel all this misery into a major aesthetic statement, *Freaks* is mannered, dirge-like, appallingly produced, and marred most of all by some strained vocals, which constantly reach for the baritone force of Scott Walker, which is not smart if you lack the pipes. *Freaks* is often embarrassing, but when it is, this isn't so much because of the uncomfortable subject matter as it is the consequence of the ineptitude of the playing, the off-key wobbles of the crooning, the barely-in-time drums. They hadn't yet learned how to make a virtue out of cheapness, out of the mismatch between opulent ambitions and straitened circumstances, or how to make misery poignant or affecting rather than merely miserable. Throughout, the songs make you feel quite awful *for them*, which means that at least on the level of communicating anguish the record is a success.

'They Suffocate at Night', improbably released as a single in 1987, is surely the summation of *Freaks*, and from the opening lines - 'his body loved her; his mind was set on other things' - there's something of a dualism problem here. 'This went on for several nights', he moans, and it sounds like it; he arrangement, with its pizzicato playing, and John Cale-like drone nearly makes it into a stark statement rather than an extended whine. The other single, 'Masters of the Universe', recasts the conflict in terms of Nietzschean fantasy – the awkward, onanistic protagonist imagines himself as ÜUbermensch as a way out of his predicament, with some powerchords for effect. 'Being Followed Home' is an eminently believable narrative of a small-town beating. It's the first time that an urban environment of any kind appears in a Pulp song, and it's as horrible as the interiors where the rest of it takes place – a 'dead seaside town', full of lurking footsteps, hands 'leaving marks in the sand' and the smell of 'piss and dead fish'. After the kicking, and after returning to consciousness, the battered protagonist collapses in the road, and spends the rest of the song lamenting over some nameless female 'you', who seems as much to blame as the seaside menfolk.

There are a couple of moments where all this unleavened

misery starts to grow into something more affecting. 'I Want You', a song which Pulp performed on their last tour in 2002, is *Freaks'* stand-out, building on the subtlety and detail of 'Little Girl (With Blue Eyes' that is otherwise so disappointingly absent from the record. Here, Jarvis is torn between hatred and need, desire and shame, and what's especially clear is that it's desire *itself* that is most worrying. The awkward croon sings of something which is irresistible but which nonetheless should be resisted, the asceticism summed up surely in the definitive, self-emasculating assertion 'you've got to stamp upon its head!' The chorus – the nearest thing *Freaks* gets to a memorable melody – is a matter of devotion and supplication, of self-abnegation and fear of literally losing an already tentative manhood; 'I'll lose myself inside you...I'll take you, I'll keep you and I'll throw myself away'. 'Don't You Know' is similarly promising, its meditation on dependency and futility constantly threatening to become a perfect tortured pop record only to throw it away in a graceless, ungainly chorus.

So why bother to sift through all of this, to examine in detail an oeuvre which is clearly a failure? Because, aside from an EP's worth of songs, everything Pulp had recorded between 1981 and 1987 showed very little sign of a group of much worth, or one who should continue to be subsidised by state or record company. In present circumstances, there's little doubt that they'd have been dropped, probably when they handed *Freaks* in, without even the chance to have it distributed by the Cartel and to be not bought in independent record shops across the country. Thankfully, because of the fact that both the indie ethos and the by-today's-standards-generous state benefits gave groups a certain freedom not just to experiment, but also *to be crap*, to make their juvenilia, make mistakes and learn from them, Pulp grew towards greatness. In fine art, something in which certain group members would soon be dabbling, this much is expected – it's difficult to list more than a handful of notable artists who didn't start off with various mis-steps and gaucheries. In pop, with its cult of youth, it's this which is the exception. And again, it's this which lay behind the explosive tensions in their 1990s work, the fact that they'd spent year upon year being ignored by the world at large; but the principal reason why they were ignored, at least at first, was because they weren't terribly good. To be fair, Pulp hardly hid this fact – the Cocker-penned sleevenotes to *Masters of the Universe* were rejected by Fire for being too scathing about his own past work.

Oh, Pitsmoor Woman!

Then, there's another sudden leap, this time into a sound which finally fits them. Until now, only 'Little Girl' and 'I Want You' had shown any signs of assurance or panache – this is indie, after all, and such things are at a premium. So the escape route was to get out of indie altogether, into its antithesis, at least at the time – Disco. 'Death Comes to Town' was recorded not long after *Freaks* was released, as a prospective single for Sheffield label Fon (who sat on it). From the first notes, the first sound of a drum machine, tilting into a morbid synthesised glam, we're dealing with an almost completely different entity to that which recorded 'They Suffocate at Night'. Two versions were recorded, one of them restructured into something between David Essex and Nitro Deluxe's 'Let's Get Brutal'. This version, 'Death Goes to the Disco', as bright and dramatic as a hit single, ended up on most of the many cash-in compilations released in 1995, fizzing and popping with 808s, analogue synths and string samples, to the point where it could be listened to alongside 'Sorted For Es and Wizz' without embarrassment. Listened to casually, with its absurdly lubricious lyrics – 'I'll take your sister...I'll take your mother as she lies in bed at night...and your brother who is busy wasting time...', the song seemed to be a matter of vengeful copulation, taken to the point of ridiculousness, much as you'd hear in a *Different Class* song like 'Pencil Skirt'. It takes place in a similar space, as our protagonist 'stalks these yellow-lit cul-de-sacs at night', but – as you realise on the third or fourth listen – the protagonist is death himself, and when he's 'taking' all these people, he's not showing them a good time. 'I want your body and I want your soul', he cries, but this revenge fantasy is more *Carrie* than *Room At the Top*. Soon after, Jarvis Cocker and bassist Steve Mackey decamp to London, to study at St Martin's College, where a less existential conflict would be formed.

The death-disco sound heard on 'Death Comes to Town' would be honed two years later in 1989, when the same group recorded the *Separations* LP (which wasn't released until 1992). The first single from the album, 'My Legendary Girlfriend', a minor indie chart hit in 1990, is a pounding disco opus, perhaps the earliest recorded instance of bedsit house. Candida Doyle's array of old synthesisers dominate here for the first time, as they will all the group's finest moments. Italo-house pianos, shimmering, swelling synth-strings, strange whines, burbles and hums at the track's threshold, all conveying an electric thrill, a cinematic sweep, that was completely absent beforehand. With half of the group out of Sheffield and living in London, the former hometown becomes the subject matter - and this is a sexualised city, where the post-industrial landscape is suffused with carnality in its every twist, turn, alleyway and precinct. The song begins with the protagonist in bed, listening to the titular girlfriend's breathing, then they wake up and take an oneiric walk through Sheffield. The temptation just to quote huge chunks of lyric here is unavoidable:

So I woke her...and we went walking through the sleeping town... down deserted streets... Frozen gardens grey in the moonlight...fences...down to the canal... Creeping slowly past cooling towers... Deserted factories...looking for an adventure... I wandered the streets calling your name... Jumping walls...hoping to see a light in the window... Let me in...let me come in...let me in tonight ... Oh I see you shivering in the garden...silver goose-flesh in the moonlight...

The strained croon is replaced by something which really, really shouldn't have worked - a breathless, spoken monologue, taken from Isaac Hayes or Barry White. Now that it's fairly familiar, we should remember just how unprecedented it actually was for a skinny, pale, indie rock singer to assume such a role completely without irony, without nudging or winking, and not only that but to pull it off, but to add a vocabulary of pants, yelps and squeals to the repertoire, which build and build to orgasmic proportions. In London, Cocker and Mackey started going to raves, but the effect of house and techno on the group was not to attempt (in the Mancunian baggy style ushered in by the Stone Roses) some sort of fusion based on lumpy funk-rock, but to take an ostensibly backwards step to the disco from which house emerged. Except here Jarvis himself takes on the Donna Summer role, he becomes himself the sex object, only a couple of years after 'They Suffocate at Night'. And what seems to drive it is the city itself, only beforehand mentioned in *Freaks'* 'Being Followed Home'. If Sheffield itself can be sexy, then so can he. But for the rest of *Separations*, when it isn't the magical space of 'My Legendary Girlfriend', Sheffield is an enemy, something that has to be defeated – 'I'm going to show this town who's master, as soon as I get off this train...'

Separations is divided into two halves, one of which continues, vastly more successfully, the tortured balladry of *Freaks*, and the other of which descends into the urbanist sexdisco of 'My Legendary Girlfriend'. The first half is still full of tales of broken relationships and anguished couples, only here with a passion (and compassion) which is completely absent from the earlier record; and they're trapped by circumstance rather than by their bodies, with 'Down by the River' or 'Don't You Want Me

Anymore?, we're in a strongly defined northern town, which one protagonist is on the verge of leaving, both pulled back and propelled forward by memory and guilt. 'She's Dead' is the centrepiece of this song-suite on internal exile. Here, a chorus of cheap synthesisers - modifying Noel Coward's quip about the 'potency of cheap music' into the sadness of cheap instruments - creates a charity shop requiem, rendering all but unbearable this tale of death in a northern town, with the overtones of kitsch not toyed with, as so many lesser lights would, but embraced - here, Jarvis is heaven's own mobile disco crooner.

The title track is nearly as fabulous, with a vertiginous moment where a huge, absurd swell of Slavic violins suddenly gives way to a tinny drum machine and the prospect of Chicory Tip soundtracking early Antonioni, aided by the new vocabulary of heavy breathing and orgasmic yelps. The second side includes one reasonably straight, not entirely successful but clumsily enjoyable Sheffield techno effort intoned by Russell Senior, 'This House is Condemned': co-produced by one of Sweet Exorcist, soon to record the monumental 'Testone', although there's not much sign of its cavernous minimalism here. Perhaps this relative failure put them off ever attempting so direct a foray into techno again, although it is implicit for much of the next ten years. Particularly so in Separations' two other disco epics, both attempting to follow the single's unlikely sublimity. 'Death II' restores the sense of tragedy to disco which the ironists had removed - this is disco in the same fashion as the bleak, dead-end world of the original *Saturday Night Fever*: 'watch my spirit melt away, down at the D-I-S-C-O'; the same story as 'How Soon Is Now', only with a grim determination to take the metronomic music for other ends, rather than glum condemnation. 'Death II' seems to catalogue some sort of attempt to break out of the world of *Freaks* and the record's first side, where he tries to 'fill his head with other women', with a world of glamour, music and sex, but is constantly pulled back by poverty, and memory, with an ignominious return home at 2am.

'Countdown' - the far superior 7" version of which is not, sadly, on the LP - is where you hear for the first time one major theme of the next few years. That is, disco as vehicle for proletarian (over)ambition, for the imperative to escape - and not just at the end of the week, but as a means of getting out, out of the provinces, out of poverty. This is melodrama as Fassbinder made it, courting ridiculousness, cruel, lurid and cheap, where the protagonist's overwhelming ego and jealousy leave only the option of self-advancement. Yet while *Saturday Night Fever* documents the more familiar working class 'Friday on my Mind' mentality of work/weekend, 'Countdown' is the disco of the dole fantasist - 'it could be tonight, oh if I ever leave this room'. And in the accompanying video, you can find, finally, someone accentuating his most absurd features in order to make himself into a superstar, in the best Warholian manner. The dancing and hand movements are to accentuate just how tall and thin he is, the effeminate yelps and breathiness court accusations of seediness, and yet it all comes off, all suddenly convinces. This is 'vengeful self-creation' of a similar, but far more ruthlessly effective manner to that of Morrissey, who after a brief moment taunting and flaunting himself at the world outside, soon opted for staying in his room, in picking over the same scabs, in a refusal to engage, a withdrawal both physical and artistic, into ever-less affecting variations on a theme. Yet instead of opting for noble defeat Pulp were clearly more interested in conquest, with all the dubiousness that entails.

2

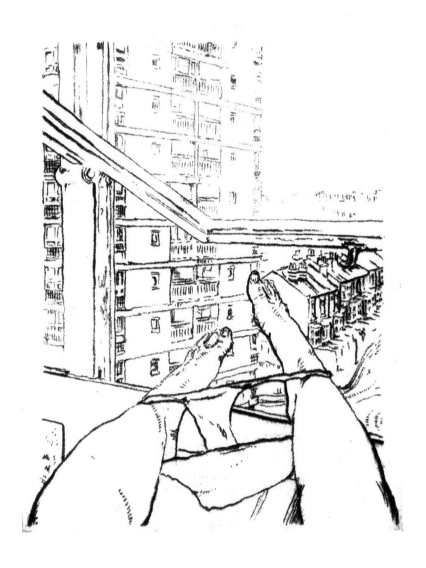

Children Conceived in the Aisles
of Meadowhall

I know the working class, the new working class, and I know their fatalism and their tiny minds. I know they believe that things were never any different from the way they are now, and I know they believe they can never be different. I know that in this country you can live and die and never meet a person from outside your social class apart from in a purely commercial context – the fellatrix, the fishmonger, the physician...I know also that working class people bring up their children without hope, with horrifically hemmed-in horizons, with a savage lack of faith. I know that for years I believed working class people inherently superior to other people, and now I know they're not and it hurts, it hurts *like hell. The working class were my religion, and I know I have lost my faith.*

Julie Burchill, 'How I Learned To Stop Worrying and Loathe the Proletariat' (1985)

The pirate radio told us what was going down

Either driving in from the M1 that traverses it or gliding along the former Midland Railway, the first sight of Sheffield is, if looked at in the abstract, stunningly beautiful. Built ('like Rome', they'll tell you) on seven hills, when you look closer you find something of somewhat deficient loveliness. As John Ruskin pointed out in the 19th century, the majestic setting of this major steeltown of the industrial revolution – the town where the steel-making process was invented, in fact – was irretrievably scarred by it, with redbrick and Yorkshire stone terraces running up its steep inclines, and gigantic, expansive, low-rise steelworks dominating its northern edges and belching smoke into its atmosphere. The smoke is long since gone, but the atmosphere is palpable. Coming in from the north, as the surviving steelworks and the replacement 'regeneration' sites – shopping malls, arenas, ice rinks – give way to the city centre, you're in the bizarre world of Attercliffe, where sex shops take up the premises of former cutlery works. Then, passing under the grandiose, stone-built Wicker Arches, the first things you notice are two enormous, ultra-modernist housing estates, clinging to the edges of the tallest two peaks – these are Park Hill and Hyde Park, one now partly a boarded-up concrete skeleton, the other clad in plastic. Walk up to these and look down, and you'll notice that some of the other hills are 'planted' with high-rise outcrops, and some others are slashed by drastic scars. Follow them, and you find the smoother, more elegant Arts Tower of Sheffield University, but follow that viewpoint further and you get to the thuggish hulk of the Hallamshire Hospital. Inbetween, a mess of concrete office blocks, tacky 2000s yuppiedromes and a handful of surviving factory chimneys act as punctuation. From an elevated point, say from the bizarre proto-space-age spike of the Victorian Cholera monument, you can see a city which looks cranky, ad hoc, cheap but still palpably futuristic. At night, like Los Angeles, it's a view of a million twinkling yellow street lights, climbing up and down the hills.

Aside from the steel, it's a city best known outside of the UK either among fans of modernist architecture – the likes of Park Hill and Hyde Park had an enormous effect on the development of public housing throughout Europe – or for various experimental pop musics. This was the home of The Human League/Heaven 17, Vice Versa/ABC, Cabaret Voltaire, Comsat Angels, and after a fallow period throughout the mid-80s, its Techno City rep – the sense it was Britain's analogue to Detroit, in the way its electronic musicians held a ruinous, dilapidated, deindustrialised present to account for its failure to create a future - was cemented when it became home to Warp Records and its early groups, the likes of Sweet Exorcist and Forgemasters. They made a stripped-down, dub-influenced techno seemingly designed to fill the empty sheds left when the steel industry departed. Less futuristically, this is the city where blues bellower Joe Cocker came from, and another Sheffield-based Cocker would occasionally claim to be his relative.

The next three Pulp singles were released on Gift Records, from 1992 to 1993, then collected by Island Records as *Intro – the Gift Recordings*. Gift was a subsidiary set up purely to release Pulp singles, run by Warp itself - who, after releasing the definitive 'Yorkshire bleep' likes of LFO's *Frequencies* and Nightmares on Wax's 'Aftermath', were then reorienting themselves to 'electronic listening music', an album-oriented genre they themselves described as a new prog rock. Warp's music videos, peculiar little things accompanying in abstract manner what rock fans then described as 'faceless techno bollocks', were often directed by Martin Wallace and former St Martin's film student Jarvis Cocker. So it's a plausible counterfactual to imagine the 1990s, and Pulp's 15 minutes of fame, if they had released these three singles on Warp proper, if they had been seen as an electronic band rather than indie-schmindie. Given that they've since besmirched their minimalist reputation by signing all manner of indie bands, including the utterly nondescript Maximo Park, they perhaps missed a trick here – the possibility of making alliances between the melodramatic pop 7" and the abstract 12", something which Broadcast, a less populist but equally songful group managed easily enough at Warp a decade later. As it is, the divide stayed.

Obviously Pulp didn't make straightforward Sheffield techno records, with the exception of the not-entirely-successful 'This House is Condemned', but you can't imagine their swerve into hysterical analogue disco from 1990-4 without the precedent of house and techno. In their evident interest in the sounds that most working class youth were actually dancing to every weekend throughout the '90s, Pulp weren't wholly unique in Britpop. Noel Gallagher, an honest chancer whose intelligence is often underrated, was, along with Pulp's members, perhaps the only ex-raver in that milieu (and Oasis were, along with Pulp, its only major working class band). Oasis' endless, all-encompassing exhortations to 'shine', make a better day, take me higher and so forth, their champagne supernovas and let's-all-hold-hands homilies, were quite transparently an application of rave's vague, all-purpose, non-specific euphoria to the pub and the muddy music festival, removing them from the more questionable spaces of the club or the orbital rave. This meaningless positivity became the perfect soundtrack to the rise of New Labour; all the vacant optimism of a eurodance hit, with none of the unnervingly druggy ambience. Pulp did something far more intriguing with these forms, though, using their least classicist possibilities, taking the expansive space, non-verse/chorus song structures, and the layers of artificial textures, and applying them to a rickety glam-disco band. It's in this, too, that they were at their most experimental. Although it was in the late '90s that they'd be found citing La Monte Young, the records where Pulp created a sound that was truly *other*, was their delirious run from 1991's 'My Legendary Girlfriend' to 1994's *Sisters* EP.

The city is a woman, bigger than any other

With the major exception of 'Common People', you can't necessarily hear this in their singles, which are perfectly structured, melodramatic three minute capsules, quintessential 7" records - 'O.U', 'Razzmatazz', 'Lipgloss', 'Babies', all of them charged yet controlled pop songs, the last three of them indie disco staples for a decade afterwards. They're all remarkable in their own way, a tactile and tacky assemblage of dreamlike textures, suggestive stabs and hysterical choruses. On 'O.U', say, you have a utopian, expansive sound, a Hillman Imp motorik fighting with a lyric of cynicism and inertia. But this stretches out into something more cinematic in the albums and in the B-Sides, through a series of partly-spoken word epics. They're not songs as such, with no verses, no choruses; and the vocals don't even entail singing as such, but a compelling series of switches from monologue, dense with minutiae – we are told in detail how his protagonists furnish their houses, what underwear they are wearing – and an improbable array of yelps, effeminate orgasmic cries, wails, whimpers. On these songs, Jarvis Cocker lurches from an elegantly precise social anatomist into an incoherent sybaritic supplicant within seconds. There are several of these pieces – after 'My Legendary Girlfriend', they continue with 'Deep Fried in Kelvin', 'Inside Susan', 'David's Last Summer', and have a final unexpected reprise with 'Wickerman' – but the best is what vies with 'Common People' and 'This is Hardcore' to be their masterpiece, 'Sheffield: Sex City', b-side to the 1992 release of 'Babies'. When I was 16, I and my girlfriend were completely obsessed with this song, and we walked around willing ourselves to see the teeming, simmering, carnal city described, peering up into the L-shaped windows of the tower blocks, past the twitching curtains of the semis, imagining the couplings and perversions inside. It also soundtracked something fairly momentous between us. It is, more than anything else, the reason why this book was written.

Jarvis intones a series of Sheffield place names, with luridly sensual relish - from 'Intake' onwards, each one of them empha-sised for any possible double-meanings. Frechville, Hackenthorpe, Shalesmoor, *Wombwell*. The next voice you hear is Candida Doyle, deadpan and Yorkshire, reading - of all things - from one of the sexual fantasies in a Nancy Friday book. Here, as in 'My Legendary Girlfriend' (to which it is, according to the sleevenotes, 'the morning after') the city itself is the focus for all libidinal energies. 'We were living in a big block of flats...within minutes the whole building was fucking. I mean, have you ever heard other people fucking, and really enjoying it? Not like in the movies, but when it's real...'. Then, the 'sun rose from behind the gasometers at 6.30am', and we're on a tour of the carnal possibilities in a post-industrial city.

The most important sounds in it (aside from Jarvis' own increasingly astonishing groans, howls, gasps and ecstatic squeals) are hers, too - the banks of synths, taken from the same jumble sale ransacked at the same time by Stereolab, interspersed with some more recent artificial instruments. It's these smears of indistinct, tinny keyboard atmospheres, the arpeggiated stutters, the repetitious house vamps and Russell Senior's queasily treated violin, which simulate the vertiginous feeling of nervousness, anticipation and mania which underpin the ridiculous, magnificent lyric, an obsessive, clammily sexual ambience. Underneath, a metronomic kick drum pounds, and deep, relentless low-end throbs, which the group got Warp's in-house engineer to lower to sub-bass levels. As it pulses, the whole city is 'getting stiff in the building heat', and Jarvis walks through its entire extent trying to find his lover. So overwhelmed is he by the sheer sexuality of Sheffield that he finds himself 'rubbing up against lamp-posts, trying to get rid of it'. The places made sexual are exemplars of non-utopian everyday life, as we traverse the semis, the gardens, and hear 'groans from a T-reg Chevette - you bet...you bet...', and in a particularly memorable moment stop to penetrate 'a crack in the pavement'. This transfigured space is cut with moments of frustrating mundanity; 'crumbling concrete bus shelters', and tedious nights indoors watching television. The pursuit is interrupted, because 'the fares went up at seven', our protagonist loses his lover while 'sentenced to three years in the housing benefit waiting room'. The frustration and fascination builds and builds and builds to the point of explosion, leaving the city's topographical extremes as location for the final consummation, with the city abstracted below them. 'We finally made it, on a hilltop at 4am. A million twinkling yellow street lights. The whole city is your jewellery box. Reach out, and take what you want...' The city has not survived its orgy, and our lovers survey the wreckage left over. 'Everyone on Park Hill came in unison at 4.13AM, and the whole block fell down. A tobacconist caught fire, and everyone in the street died of lung cancer.'

This tumultuous collapse was our favourite moment in the song, and we always imagined it taking place in the vast slab block which loomed over this particular courtship (did they have similar fantasies, looking down on us?). It was a bit of a revelation a few years later when, developing what was then a part-time interest in architecture, I found out just how famous and important Park Hill was, and saw photographs of this enormous, snaking collective housing estate, with its wide streets in the sky, its interconnecting decks thrusting out of each block, its form rising to different storeys depending on its place on the hill; the longest walkway has for the last few years had the graffito 'I LOVE YOU, MARRY ME', as if in tribute to 'Sheffield: Sex City' itself. It was absolutely perfect, a visual emblem of the familiar 1960s-built city turned into a utopian, libidinal megastructure.

We were living in a pretty typical, symptomatic English urban space, where Victorian terraces and 1930s semis are right next to vast 1960s council estates. Because of this proximity, it was a deeply class-conscious place, with everyone eager to differentiate themselves from each other, to allot one area as 'common', another as 'posh', another as a sink estate beyond the pale. So the other major urbanist song on *Intro* was, if not as world-shattering an experience as 'Sheffield: Sex City', something which seemed to describe our environment equally aptly: 'Styloroc (Nites of Suburbia)'. The detritus of the 70s was everywhere, in the many, many local charity shops and in the seldom-updated furnishings of our rented houses, and here all that past-its-sell-by date detritus was imagined as something richly perverse - black hair, sprouting beneath bri-nylon underwear. The song actually dates, rather amazingly, from the 'Little Girl' era, but appears here as a cranky yet sweeping Stylophone epic, reimagining that obsolete early synthesiser as an instrument whose rough tactile scratch is like acrylics on sweating flesh.

The lyric is more mordant than the ecstatic 'Sex City', pitching itself as a vicarious tour through a 'strange land', and it's this curtain-twitching that leads to the accusations of voyeurism, seediness and so forth that are usually attendant on discussions of Jarvis Cocker's view of sex. We didn't take it as such. It was far more a way of making the city and suburbia interesting, of making our (built) environment and the people in it more than a random collection of buildings and people tediously grafting - we knew that in fact they were pulsating with intrigue behind the fences, at the end of the plazas and above the hedges. Quite possibly, we had to believe it in order not to give way to the consumerist tedium which was then remaking our city. We were fascinated by the 'thousand fake orgasms every night, behind thick draylon curtains', and listened out for them. Regardless of whatever we took from these songs and imposed on a Southern city, it's also here that a certain retrospection comes in. If it's not nostalgia in the traditional sense, then it's the now-familiar trope of 'nostalgia for the future', in which Pulp were paradoxically ahead of the game by a decade or so, with these city songs predating its theoretical formulation in Svetlana Boym's *The Future of Nostalgia*. It's predicated not so much on what Sheffield was, but what it could have been.

A 'Guide to Sheffield' that Pulp did for *NME* in 1993 partly concentrates on its role as centre of the 'Socialist Republic of South Yorkshire', when the red flag famously flew above the town hall. This comes out in a particularly quotidian way through these songs, where the all-but-free public transport is recalled as a way of seeing the city as a totality, only to be destroyed with deregulation and privatisation: 'I remember when the buses were only 10p to go anywhere. That's why buses are mentioned quite a lot in our songs. Anyway, it all stopped in the mid-'80s. There are about six different bus companies now, like Eager Beaver, Yorkshire Terrier...it's ridiculous - if the driver sees the stop they're supposed to be going to hasn't got any people at it, they change the number and go to one that has. People came from Japan to see our bus service - it was the end of the Western World.' As much as Pulp's Sheffield songs were the voyeur's view into an interior, they were an all-surveying view from the top deck of a bus.

More particularly, their gazetteer is about the city's failure to become the modernist metropolis that it once promised to be. Of all provincial cities, Sheffield went furthest towards becoming some sort of viable modern city, reconstructing itself after the Blitz in a markedly dramatic form, using its topography – this is a city practically built into the Peak District – as an advantage. At one end, there was the slickness of Sheffield University, designed by Gollins Melvin Ward (in a style completely in hock to Mies van der Rohe) in the early 1960s, the first wholly Modernist University campus in the UK. This series of precisely engineered, machine-tooled, glass-and-steel pavilions and towers, recently renovated to their post-war splendour, is closer to the high modernist aesthetic of Warp, rather than Pulp's more Heath Robinson pop modernism. To find the possible inspirations for that, you have to look elsewhere, first to the Castle Square 'Hole in the Road', an underpass-cum-shopping-centre, whose early 1990s demolition was lamented by Pulp in the music press as an attempt 'to make everything like Meadowhall', the postmodernist out-of-town mall constructed on the site of a former steelworks; or you could find it in a series of montage-based modernist edifices designed under the City Architect J.L Womersley, constructed as assemblages of walkways, multiple levels and almost kitsch details. There's the Castle Market, for one, where Cocker worked on the fish stall in his youth, the subject of a short local TV item where he held it up as an example of what makes Sheffield unique and specific. Then there's the housing estates, the monumental, interconnected collective housing blocks placed on the city's hilltops. Park Hill, we know about; but there's also its successors, Hyde Park and Kelvin, the latter of which gets a markedly less ecstatic Pulp song devoted to it. There's a suburban version, Gleadless Valley, a vision of hilltop modernism full of oddly-shaped houses and flats built into the landscape according to the tenets of picturesque planning. It's here that Russell Senior was raised.

Read another guide, any Shell Guide or Pevsner from the 1960s or 1970s, and it's this which they will tell you to look for – aside from a single Georgian square and a couple of Victorian civic buildings, they all point the traveller to that visionary series of housing estates and markets, or to a new town hall designed as a concrete honeycomb and soon nicknamed 'the egg box'. This vision was propagandised in books – *Sheffield: Emerging City* or *Ten Years of Housing in Sheffield*, which was translated into French and Russian – and into a propaganda film, *Sheffield: City on the Move*, a confident, convincing, if undeniably clunky vision of civic futurism that was sampled as a 'what were we thinking!' joke at the start of the 'dance, prole, dance' genre's most noted product, *The Full Monty*. Many schemes were shelved for lack of money - at one point, the council were making plans to run street decks and walkways across the entire Sheaf Valley. By the 1990s, buildings that had a lifespan of barely 20 years, whose futurism was suddenly dated – the aforementioned Town Hall, the 'wedding cake' registry office next to it, the concrete housing estates of Broomhall, Hyde Park and Kelvin – began to be demolished, leaving huge scars across the city which haven't fully healed two decades later.

Another early 1990s *NME* interview makes it especially clear just how much of an effect this construction and destruction had on the future members of Pulp: "Sheffield's full of half-arsed visions of cities of the future that turn into a pile of rubbish,' Russell Senior reflects, standing on the biggest traffic round-about in Europe. 'We grew up reading the local paper and seeing 'Sheffield, city of the future,' with a map of how it's going to be and pictures of everyone walking around in spacesuits, smiling. But we're the only ones who took it seriously...' 'When I was younger I definitely thought I'd live in space," says Jarvis Cocker ruefully. 'But when you realise you're not going to, it colours your life; you can't think, 'It's alright if I'm signing on because I'll be on Mars soon', you have to try and get it down here.' What runs through all of this is the lament of true believers in modernism, holding the present to account for its failure to create a viable future, and the pinched vision of the possible that then instils in those born after the future; as Cocker would yelp in 1998, obliquely apropos New Labour's workfare schemes, 'we were brought up on the space race - *now they expect you to clean toilets'*. *Intro* opens with a song that confronts this directly, 'Space', where an ambient drift of indeterminate hums and flutters imagines the previously longed-for journey above the earth's surface, where all the trash of bedsit life is left behind – 'this is what you've been waiting for', he whispers, 'no dust collecting in corners or cups of tea that go cold before you drink them...it doesn't matter if the lifts don't work or the car won't start. We're going to escape' - and then suddenly rejects the reverie, stiffening into a determination to 'get my kicks down below'.

No-one ever really got inside Susan

It's this that lies behind all the obvious retro sounds and signi-fiers - the Farfisas, Stylophones and Moogs, the jumble sale clothes, the tower blocks, space hoppers and luridly bright artificial fabrics that pervade the videos - a sense of being cheated out of the future, responding by fetishising the last time that a viable future appeared to exist. Yet the songs do delve into 1970s nostalgia, not least as a way of talking about the stripped-pine compromises and bland conformities of the 1990s. You can hear this especially vividly in 'Inside Susan - A Story In Three Parts', which concludes the Gift singles and B-sides collected on *Intro*. This tale of a 'Rotherham puberty' followed by 'wild teen years in Sheffield' and eventual middle-class stability in Camberwell, is another example of Jarvis' obsessive/sympathetic studies of women, although here with a detail and wit that shouldn't obscure how it eventually ends up, as they so often do from this point, to be about whether or not she'll sleep with the narrator. The first, 'Stacks' is Pulp at their most straightforwardly retro, albeit with the 70s parts all assembled in the wrong order. It's cheap, fizzing, and absolutely riven with nostalgia, all sports halls, gropings on the bus and 'sky blue trainer bras'. It's an enormously enjoyable bit of tat, but rather pales in comparison with 'Inside Susan', the centrepiece of the story.

The only obvious precedent for songs like this, with their detail and sympathy for their mundane protagonists elevating them into something almost mythical, is Scott Walker circa 'Plastic Palace People', a flu-accompanied hearing of which inspired Cocker to try and write like this in the first place - but even the likes of 'Montague Terrace (In Blue)' were never as sharp in their detail as this. Dispensing with actual singing of any sort, bar a refrain of muffled gasps and cries, this is all monologue, over a dense, bright, vividly exciting motorik pulse which intensifies at key moments in the plotless narrative. It's a bus travelogue, and develops according to where the bus is at any given point, sparking off Susan's alternately bored or intrigued thoughts, with the most mundane details easily transformed into surreal re-imagining:

The bus is waiting on the High Street when it suddenly begins to rain torrentially, and it sounds like someone has emptied about a million packets of dried peas onto the roof of the bus. "What if it just keeps raining?", she thinks to herself. "And it was just like being in an aquarium except it was all shoppers and office workers that were floating past the windows instead of fish."

As the bus drives on, she thinks of a party where she was hit on by 'some German exchange students who were very immature', and finally wonders: "maybe this bus won't stop, and I'll stay on it until I'm old enough to go into pubs on my own, and it'll drive me to a town where people with black hair are treated specially, and I can make lots of money from charging fat old men five pounds a time to look up my skirt, and they'll be queuing up to take me out to dinner'. Daniel Clowes' *Ghost World* is, more than any other work of the time, closely comparable, an awkward, urbane man's idea of a melancholic teenage girlhood marked by attempts to romanticise the mundane; his Enid Coleslaw is a curtain-twitcher and only ostensibly cynical dreamer desperately attempting to resist the compromises of adulthood who could easily be found relocated to South Yorkshire in these songs. And much as Enid is an anagrammatic cipher for Clowes himself, Susan could easily be a feminised version of her creator. The song ends in bitterness at the reactions of others towards Susan - 'they put her in a corner and let her heat up the room, warming their hands and backsides in front of her, and then slagging her off around town.'

This bitterness continues in '59 Lyndhurst Grove'. She's managed to get out of Yorkshire (like the narrator), and is now enjoying a comfortable but loveless existence with an architect in south London. The scornful lyric, partly delivered in a heart-broken but sly falsetto - is the first essay in what will become a major theme, the sexual politics of domestic interiors. 'There's a picture by his first wife on the wall. Stripped floorboards in the kitchen and the hall...they were dancing with children round their necks, talking business, books and records, art and sex. All things being considered, you'd call it a success, you wore your black dress.' The sound is very close to Stereolab's use of antiquated easy listening as a metonym for decadence and obsolescence, a droning Moog Muzak that evokes both the *Romantic Moog* albums of an earlier period of domestic conformity, sounding like a sad echo of the synthetic excitement in 'Inside Susan'. Here, Susan snatches whatever fun she can in this stifling yet successful environment ('oh he's an architect, and such a lovely guy...') by embarking on an affair with someone presumably rather more exciting, a role that Jarvis will assume many times in the next few years, Regardless, in a neat gesture, Jarvis himself claimed in the sleevenotes that the whole thing was motivated by jealousy anyway - 'I played these songs to Susan the other day - she just laughed and said I was being spiteful because she wouldn't sleep with me when we first met. She also said to tell you that she's perfectly happy where she is at the moment, thank you very much.' The injury was compounded in 'The Babysitter', a 1994 b-side where Susan enviously obsesses over a teenage acquaintance welcomed into her home.

These regrets are, on the song and film 'Do You Remember The First Time?', captured in a more forgiving manner. Released in early 1994, its all-important proviso - 'I can't remember a worse time' – was a counter to any accusations of uncomplicated nostalgia, something which couldn't quite have been said about the video. In *When Surface Was Depth*, Bracewell makes great play of just how ugly the 1970s is in actual archive film, the ungain-liness of the clothes, the paste pallor of the complexions – but here, as a cute camera effect continuously circles over them, all these boys and girls embarking on their first experience are obscenely good looking. In fact, a few of them look like members of Menswear. Much more interesting, then, is the accompanying film, made for telly and – like some of Pulp's better music videos – directed by Martin Wallace and Jarvis Cocker. When not discussing class with Greek sculpture students, Cocker was at St

Martin's to study film, and as much as you can tell from his own work, the film that had a major effect on him was John Smith's *Girl Chewing Gum*, (1976) a static, verite shot of a street which a 'director' purports to direct, although it soon becomes clear that he's only trying to impose order on the general mundane chaos around him. Its combination of structuralism – of bringing attention to the film-making process itself - and self-debunking humour defines *Do You Remember The First Time?*

Put unromantically, this is a series of famous-ish talking heads discussing the loss of their virginity, and an unkind eye could see in it the nostalgia shows of the 1990s, *I heart losing my virginity in 1973*. It begins with the shot of a patch of grass, and a familiar South Yorkshire voice, explaining in minute detail what surrounds it; a dilapidated greenhouse, a high privet hedge enclosing on three sides, 'a museum with relics from Sheffield's industrial past', and a bandstand boarded up due to persistent vandalism. This, we're told, is where the director lost his virginity, and we return regularly to this patch of grass as the film continues; at one point, a worm slithers up it. The virginity-loss is cherished, not because it was some sort of orgasmic explosion, but 'because it was a secret between two people'; and maybe a hint of that secret is continued at the end, when our narrator reveals that we're not looking at the patch of grass in question, but a grass verge in front of Clapham Common tube station...Meanwhile, the interviews are interspersed with vaguely erotic static shots of construction work, and a series of suggestive road signs (most memorably, 'Crooked Usage'). The interviewees' reactions vary wildly. Interestingly, Vic Reeves and Bob Mortimer, soon-to-be the leering, thigh-rubbing hosts of the quintessentially Britpop show *Shooting Stars*, are by far the most uncomfortable, the first making nervous, unfunny jokes, the other visibly squirming in his seat. The failure of the event to live up to expectations is nearly a constant; Jo Brand remembers her head bashing against a cistern, and the sheer social discomfort afterwards ('I didn't know what the social etiquette was...do you want a cup of tea?'). What really makes the film, aside from the wit of its construction, is the artist Donald Parsnips, who lost his virginity at 26 ('it took a long time, because of my problem') and is still wide-eyed and ecstatic with relief and joy; the encounter on a wooden pallet in a squat was 'the most amazing thing that has ever happened to me. *Ever*. It was Blakean...if I had a football rattle and a scarf, I'd have ran out into the street and told everybody'. Unlike *Shooting Stars* and its ilk, there's nothing *Carry-On* about the film, no nudging, winking and leering. It speaks, affectionately and without judgement or nostalgia, of an act eventually defined as 'necessary'.

Adultery & Interiors

His 'N' Hers, where Pulp first start to achieve some kind of public prominence, is perhaps the only pop record which largely purports to be about domestic interiors. Or at least, uses them as a metaphor for sex, class and the usual things which are latent or blindingly obvious in the commodity form. It exists in a similar landscape to the Martin Parr photographs for the BBC's *Signs of the Times* book/documentary, of matching towel sets, ornamented light switches, of carefully chosen signifiers of individuality which end up as signifiers of conservatism and conformism, of status and success. Why, as you might wonder when listening to something like 'Pink Glove' or the song 'His 'n' Hers', does the 1990s bourgeois interior elicit these hysterical fits of denial and arousal? Partly, by all means, it's because of their role in working-class surrender, the kind of furnishings brought in after right-to-buy, little knick-knacks and pieces of tat introduced in order to set yourself apart, in order to proclaim to any visitor that you're no longer *Common* – the worthless trinkets that proved just how easily we were bought. Alternately, it's the obsessive tidiness of the bourgeois, the sort of obsessed-over living room described 60 years earlier in Walter Benjamin's essay 'Experience and Poverty', where any breakage, any spillage, any rearrangement of the accumulated objects, could 'wipe out the traces of their time on earth'. Benjamin proposes instead a programme of destruction to usher in a 'glass culture' of clarity and modernity – but that's not really likely with these collectors of old keyboards and clothes, the mountains of charity shop bumph that run through Pulp's mid-90s videos and sleeves, all of them mined for their overlooked, esoteric or recherché properties – instead, minimalism, the 'poor-is-cool' style seems a likelier culprit. Sometimes it's an disgust with the accumulation of commodities, sometimes disgust with accumulating the wrong kind of commodities. There's a constant tension between them, not falling into the 'my goodness, ducks on the wall!' responses that Parr sometimes courts, but never entirely definable either. But mainly, with this character – how much this corresponds to the actual tastes of Jarvis Cocker is between him and his analyst - it's because all this crap *turns him on*, reluctantly or otherwise.

This is all filtered through a perverse, 70s-damaged fixation on the erotic properties of the artificial fabrics of an earlier era. What we have here is a suburban record, where *Intro* was mostly vividly urban, and one marked by all the boredom and frustration that entails. The sleevenote communique (these rousing messages started to appear on Pulp singles from 1993 on, implying that there were now, as one zine had it, *Pulp People*, who were offered various proclamations of encouragement) links together the smugness of coupledom, the horror of interiors and the awesome tedium of the shopping malls that replaced the futurist city that was keenly and distortedly remembered on the earlier singles. The slower songs on here - 'Happy Endings', or 'Someone like the Moon', both based, 'Inside Susan'-style, on the thoughts of bored women dreaming of escape - sound as if they're coming out of some kind of supermarket tannoy, with the four-note synth chimes in the latter seeming to precede an announcement, 'could Mr Cocker come to the checkout please...', while Ed Buller's extremely underrated, cavernous, reverb-drenched production delineates the vast ennui-filled space of an out-of-town Asda.

It's a beautifully produced record, precisely for how far from 'live' it sounds, how little it resembles any kind of rock music. With a collection of antique synths (eight of them, from Korg to EMS, according to the credits) wafting around a huge, airy space, Buller's piling on of effects intersects with the keyboards to create some breathtaking moments - the first few seconds of 'Do You Remember The First Time?', where the whines and chirps of the antique machines flutter with all the quivering nervousness of a teenage couple tentatively asking each other the pointed question, the wall of synthnoise that opens the lust-crazed pulse of 'She's a Lady', the hopeless, longing swirls that waft around 'Have You Seen Her Lately?', evoking jumble sales held in the worn concrete and glass vestibules of modernist churches. Odd moments and riffs abound, such as the echoed children singing at the start of 'Acrylic Afternoons'; itself one of the strangest tracks on a deeply strange record - another slab of sexdisco, although here punctuated with high-pitched squeals which take this approach even further from its eventual roots in, say, Isaac Hayes. All this effeminacy, Jarvis as Donna Summer orgas-matron, is dedicated to a scenario where he is the bit of rough, the bit on the side of, a suburban housewife. This isn't necessarily as part of some bit of 'Mr Jones'-bashing, but based on a disassoci-ation between the surrounding objects - the acrylics, the 'pink quilted eiderdown', the settee with the TV humming in the background, and the table set for tea for when the children come home - and the act taking place underneath. The atmosphere is feverish, delirious, a tea-fuelled bacchanalia where the stifling, overfurnished suburban living room becomes a claustrophobic, overheated space of sexual obsession.

'She's a Lady', 'Lipgloss' and 'Pink Glove' continue in this vein, the making-sexy of all manner of quotidian tat, with the protagonist alternately attracted and repelled by the parapher-nalia of suburban eroticism, almost always from an outsider's perspective, either looking in on the relationships of others or as an invasive interlocutor into the exurbs and cul-de-sacs. 'She's a Lady' is especially torrid, enlivened by the frustration and resentment of 'Countdown' - while not obsessing over the lady of the title, the protagonist is staying in bed all day, moaning about 'all this crap that holds me down'. What ends up happening is that this world, with all its ambiguities and dubiousness ('I don't know why you pretend that it causes you pain', etc etc) becomes something deeply exciting, the model of adolescent fantasies. Certainly the world of 'Lipgloss', for all its vicious cuckolding and wasted lives, seemed enormously glamorous to a generation of provincial youth – to live on lipgloss and cigarettes sounded exciting rather than tawdry. Or both.

With that promise in mind, there's an intriguing change between the two videos made for 'Babies' – one by Jarvis Cocker and Martin Wallace for Gift/Warp, in 1992, the other in 1994 by Pedro Romhanyi for Island. The first is full of the structuralist jokes that pervade most of their self-made films, intertitles, jumpcuts, deliberate continuity errors and gawky, awkward actors, who look authentically 1970s in their clumsiness and sartorial inelegance; the second is full of the beautiful people, again in 1970s garb but this time seamless, all much more shiny and sexy than was ever possible. You can feel them starting to let go of the 'freaks' at this point, moving towards a more unrecon-structed notion of glamour. Wallace/Cocker's 1993 video for 'Lipgloss' catches this somewhere inbetween, still closer to struc-turalism than *TFI Friday*. The extraordinary set is a series of practically gynaecological plastic tunnels, a multicoloured total environment designed for polymorphous perversity, seemingly pulled from the imaginings of 1960s paper architects Archigram. Here is the usual 'band playing in a room', though interspersed with scenes of the woman the song is being addressed to. Both the band and the actress hold up a series of self-contradicting captions – 'Sex Interest', I Don't Exist' 'I Sing', 'I'm Shy' or 'Does This Turn You On?', while she pouts, applies lipgloss and a series of wigs.

Here too, the physical presence of the frontman is fully formed; all the (socially and bodily) crippling ailments and/or qualities visible around the time of *Freaks* are suddenly becoming sexy. There's no doubt whatsoever that this is a conscious choice; with a physicality and a countenance this awkward, all long ungainly limbs, thin, sulky lips, tiny, seedy eyes, it's as if it poses a question – what can you *do* with a body like this? It's not the possessed body of rock myth that you can see fluttering its fingers and throwing its stringly limbs into the air in these videos, not the elemental unconscious performance of an Ian Curtis or an Iggy Pop. It's the answer to the question of what can be done with these disadvantages – as if he was forced to physically rethink himself. And intentionally or otherwise, its immediate distinctiveness provided a series of stock gestures and trademarks to be easily parodied by more or less successful TV satirists.

Their other video from the time, for 'Razzmatazz', also finds them at the point where they're still able to create their own version of glamour, by equal measure tawdry and thrilling – the song's subject, a dole fantasist creating an imaginary Hollywood lovelife in order to escape facing up to a reality of poverty and inertia, is personified in an elegantly dressed and made-up young woman wandering disconsolately around a room full of rotten tea bags and a sink full of corn flakes, nibbling on 'A Touch of Class' chocolates, while the band themselves perform in front of neon lights on the streets of Paris. It's more than a little unfair that all this dreaming indolence is personified by a woman, given how much 'Razzmatazz' sounds like autobiographical self-accusation. The artwork from 1993-4 also attempts some kind of awkward, charity shop version of high glamour; 'Lipgloss', 'First Time', *His 'N' Hers* and *Sisters* were all the work of The Designers Republic, the Sheffield firm who also created Warp's sleeves; their ostentatiously elegant sans serifs frame airbrushed paintings by Philip Castle, leaving the group preserved in aspic, resplendent in their shagpile and acrylic.

This frozen glamour doesn't make the couplings any less heated. These songs are marked both by a fierce erotic fascination, with women's clothes, make-up, and obviously with sex itself (all combined in 'She's a Lady's gasped 'she wore her body back to front') and some ferocious put-downs, whether they're put into the mouths of particular characters or not: 'Lipgloss' pivots on a woman too scared to leave the house in case other women notice 'that your stomach looks bigger and your hair is a mess, and your eyes are just holes in your face'. Here, women manipulate men and vice versa, as in 'Pink Glove's tragicomic fetishism, where a singer known for his love of rayon and brinylon sneers 'it's hard to believe that you go for that stuff - baby doll nighties, synthetic fluff...' The magnificent 'Street Lites', the kind of song the lesser Britpoppers would have killed for, thrown away on a b-side, is one of the most shiveringly erotic things they recorded, featuring yet more illicit sex, more revelling in guilt - 'it wouldn't be the same, if we didn't know it was wrong', but this time, rather than a Sheffield tower block or a suburban cul-de-sac, we're in the capital, a shimmering, neon-lit vision of London seen from the back of a taxi couriering illicit liasons, far from the album's suburban Sheffield; in fact, aside from those abstract, twinkling yellow street lights, we don't even know where we are, except in a compulsive space of obsession deliberately separated from *His & Hers'* smug domesticity - 'I don't want to live with you or anywhere near you. I want to take you unawares'.

The Sisters EP – a cash-in rerelease of 'Babies' bundled with three new songs, and their first thing resembling a 'hit' - is this version of the group, the Spectorian stylophonic glam-pop group of *Separations, Intro* and *His 'N' Hers* as opposed to the mostly more conventional Chris Thomas-produced thing which followed, reaching some kind of climax. It is three songs, 'Seconds', 'Your Sister's Clothes', 'His 'N' Hers', which pass in a blur of flickering electronics, words lingered over for every possible innuendo, yearning choruses and almost tossed-off one-liners ('Seconds', with its rhyming of 'your brother/unmarried mother/another on the way', is probably the kind of throwaway he would later refer to as 'just another song about single mothers and sex', but you should never trust an artist's opinion on his own work). It's 'His 'N' Hers', the unused title track for the album, that is most gobsmacking. 'One man's fear of domestic interiors set to music' according to the sleevenotes, it's a 'Popcorn' keyboard canter driven by a pre-orgasmic synth whine. Here, we are again in suburban Sheffield, and a scenario of class conflict expressed through sex and domestic interiors: 'I wanna wipe you down, and lick the smile off your face...Though we know that it's wrong: towel sets, matching combs...oh it looks so good but does it turn you on?' The track is deeply uncomfortable, queasy, with moans and wails of excitement and disgust punctuating, rising into the guiltily ecstatic chorus, where IKEA instructions become sexual commands - 'pull the units down!' 'shove it in sideways!' It all spills over into comedy when the unnerved narrator, led by his clearly more assured bourgeois lover, is asked what he's so afraid of, leading to a litany of '90s middle-class tat: 'Belgian chocolates, James Dean posters, endowment plans, figurines, 26" screens'...and her straightforward response – 'are you stupid?' she said' - is to put his hand somewhere intimate. We leave the scene with a cry of guilty ecstasy, and his defeat.

Mister, we just want your car

This is developed from an earlier song called 'Frightened', later included on the reissue of *His 'N' Hers*, rewriting its frantic rejection into a self-abnegating embrace. The fear of the middle classes and their design choices is not the only terror here. It would be incomplete to concentrate just on the libidinous and scathing portrayals of middle class life in these songs, as there are others which talk about lumpen proletarian habits and mores with much the same ambiguity and disgust. 'Deep Fried in Kelvin', the B-side to 'Lipgloss, is like a ten-minute reversal of 'Sheffield: Sex City'. Like the latter, it centres on one of the three huge collective housing blocks designed by Jack Lynn & Ivor Smith for Sheffield City Council. Park Hill got Grade II listed and undergoes an Urban Splash-led regeneration/gentrification, Hyde Park got part-demolished, part-reclad - but the apparently identical Kelvin Flats, approvingly mentioned in the Human League's sleevenotes for the sublime 'Dancevision', were demolished in the 1990s and replaced by low-rise, low-density Barratt Homes, the sort you could imagine housing the soap-on-a-rope sagas of 'His & Hers'. In marked contrast with 'Sheffield: Sex City', there's little interest in the utopian possibilities of brutalist megastructures in 'Deep Fried', which instead depicts a people congenitally unable to live in anything other than houses with gardens, centring on a man destroying his flat by filling it with soil, trying to turn it into a garden, walking 'on promenade with concrete walkways, where pigeons go to die'. It's a vision of a consumerist, barely literate proletariat destroyed by Thatcherism, where children are 'conceived in the toilets of Meadowhall'. It has equal disdain both for the 'fizzy orange and chips' youth of this 'ghetto' and for those who might improve it (memorably, 'we don't need your sad attempts at social conscience based on taxi rides home at night from exhibition openings. We just want your car radio and bass reflex speakers. Now'), and eventually the contempt seems to be aimed at the narrator himself and his social concern.

'Joyriders', a portrait of bovine maleness like 'Dogs are

Everywhere' sharpened up, excises the angst over exactly who is speaking, as the bored teenagers are now in the first person. It's difficult to say, though, whether it's all satire or a genuine expression of class disdain - 'we can't help it, we're so thick we can't think - can't think of anything, but shit, sleep and drink'. The bleakest of all of these songs of working class boredom and casual violence/idiocy is 'Mile End', palatably translated into genial space-skiffle. Here it's the old East End, repository for Blur's proleface sentimentality, which is, when surveyed from the top of a tower block as the 'pearly king of the isle of Dogs', 'just like heaven, if it didn't look like hell', and where maintaining your difference, rather than blending in, is the only way to keep sane. 'Nobody wants to be your friend, cos you're not from round here, oh no – as if that wasn't something to be proud about!' They're all songs that appear, to the untrained eye, more or less autobiographical, tales of dole life when you could still get a council flat without having to lose an arm or a leg or have a family in double figures. Sometimes these London estates become neither utopian nor dystopian, but have a more everyday romanticism; Jarvis Cocker & Martin Wallace's elegantly self-deconstructing 1992 video to 'Babies', for instance, takes place in Southwark Council Architects' Department's Sceaux Gardens Estate, Camberwell, where Jarvis and Steve Mackey were living at the time, and like Park Hill somewhere with much architectural rep when it was built. Its low and high-rise curtain-walled blocks, with their elegant, cubic green panels and their Francophone names, were spread across green space taken over from former back gardens and overgrown bombsites. Ian Nairn wrote of Sceaux Gardens in 1966 that because of this, 'the magical transformation has happened, an estate transformed into a place'. The block named 'Voltaire' gets a particularly wry shot in the video, as do the patches of green and swaying flowers in front of the towers, creating a place perfect for the song's rum, giddy nostalgia. One of the blocks caught fire in 2009, killing several people. Some investigators blamed the council for installing as-cheap-as-possible UPVC windows on the whole block, melting in the heat, spreading the fire.

Pulp's contradictory balancing of class pride and disgust at what the working class has been reduced to is burlesqued in an unreleased song called 'Catcliffe Shakedown', on the subject of a deadzone between Sheffield and Rotherham where the group had their rehearsal rooms. It's lists various kinds of depressing stupidity to the point where it constantly seems about to collapse into laughter, clearly reproducing stuff they've either heard in the pubs or heard shouted at them as they no doubt pranced around the place looking ridiculous; 'what you looking at? Am I so beautiful?' 'You and whose army? Me, me and my fisty' 'Have a meal in a glass!' Surveying the wasteland, he incredulously asks 'they were going to build an airport here, can you imagine it? Why not stock up on string, or sample some of our duty-free parking?' Then it shifts into another, guiltier register entirely:

The film now cuts to reveal who's watching this docu-drama – a middle-class couple sit in wonder as the titles roll. All the nicotine stains and beer bellies in this film were real.

These council flat dystopias are, for all their justified bitterness, the correlate of the failed utopia that is longingly re-imagined in 'My Legendary Girlfriend' and 'Sheffield: Sex City', indicators of what has happened to the working class after (then only 15 years of) Thatcherism. If Oasis took this and played up to it, constantly stressing just how bovine they were, how they might look aggressive, might lamp you in the pub but were no threat otherwise, Pulp were something far more alarming - literate, articulate and increasingly furious. They were also far more directly unnerving to those with actual privilege; in *The Last Party*, Blur's Alex James, who nowadays runs a Marie Antoinette-style 'farm' and carouses with David Cameron, recalls 'in a lot of ways, Pulp were even bigger cunts than Oasis. They were in our birds' knickers: devious little fuckers. We definitely tried to help them...but they never had a kind word for us. I kind of object to them more than Oasis, actually. At least Oasis said 'we're going to shag your bird'. There was something a bit snidey about Pulp'. Think about that, listen to that tone – the sneaky little proles, not only were they driven by bestial urges, not only did they not know their place, but they had the unforgivable nerve to be *clever* about it too! In this dubious, pyrrhic sense at least, the enemy were thoroughly rattled; but whether true or not, it also implies that, at worst, these songs are about women being utilised as trophies in a war between men. Yet the unstoppable urge to get out, to escape one's 'place', while very different to the latter's dreams of Champagne Supernovas and guitar-shaped swimming pools, leads to its own uncomfortable contradictions and outbreaks of sheer, resentful rage. As well it might.

3

A Case of Haves Against Haven'ts

Story by Michael Blakemore about Albert Finney, who told it to him. When Albert made his million on Tom Jones *and went on his sabbatical trip around the world, he stopped in Acapulco. One evening he was drinking Dom Perignon on a balcony with the most beautiful girl in Mexico. He took her into the bathroom and put his cock into her. With every thrust, he said, out loud: 'That's for Dad, and* that's *for Mum, and* that's *for Uncle Ted, and* that's *for Cousin Jim, and* that's *for Auntie Marron...' A whole working-class family shared that fuck.*

Kenneth Tynan, *Diaries*, 9th January 1973

There is a war in Progress

In 1995, Pulp's merchandisers started selling a glaring orange and bright green T-Shirt – its colour-clashing design based on a second-hand shirt worn by Candida Doyle in the 'Mis-Shapes' video – with the legend *'I'm Common'*. The word is used here as a badge of allegiance, as a statement of some kind of class pride; a kind of solidarity. It wasn't especially well-made, and the orange collar had a tendency to get very limp. Yet in interviews around the same time, Jarvis Cocker pointed out that *common* was, for him, an insult, a way of dismissing people as some kind of nondescript pov mass. Common, when used by the (usually petit, usually close enough to falling into the proletariat to be very keen on such stark differentiation) English bourgeois, means proletarian, means a panoply of related things from poor, to benefit-claiming, to vulgar and slovenly, to 'no better than she ought to be'. It means undiscriminating, drawn to the tacky, and most likely preoccupied with low pleasures, such as an immoderate fondness for food, hedonism, or sex. The song exists somewhere inbetween these two views.

Which makes it all the more instructive in political terms that 'common' also means 'collective', in the old Labour/Good Old Cause sense of England as a 'Commonwealth' as opposed to a Monarchy, and most of all in the common lands, the agricultural commons that were owned by nobody, free spaces that were forcibly destroyed by the enclosures of the late eighteenth century, leading to persistent outbreaks of resistance – the burning of country houses, the smashing of machinery, the issuing of luridly bloodthirsty letters signed by General Ludd or Captain Swing – until those who favoured the commons were starved into newly expanding industrial cities like Sheffield. So to be common is also to have little interest in property, an unforgivable lapse in the value system of the English middle classes; to be a mass susceptible to moments of *jacquerie* and insurrection. In terms of botanic classification meanwhile, common is a synonym more for 'uninteresting' – common or garden, commonly occurring, easily and frequently found, the opposite of 'exotic'.

This switching between interlinked meanings is a reminder of just how furious with resonance 'Common People' actually is. In the 1990s, class was reduced to a univalent thing, something which has continued in the 2000s – a 'white working class' conceived as an identity, an ethnicity, and no longer defined by its actual economic status. It's a matter of signifiers, in which Alan Sugar is indisputably working class because of how he speaks, for the barrow-boy coarseness of his accent; but in which call centre workers, no matter how extreme their exploitation, are 'white collar' and hence indisputably middle class. 'Common People' is a matter of class conceived as, as they would put it in 'I Spy', 'a case of haves against haven'ts', as antagonism between those who 'succeed' and those who do not, between those whose lives are mapped out in advance as public school-university-the professions (or more likely today, PR and media), or as school-unemployment-dead-end job, something which persists today more virulently than ever before, no matter how much the odd ex-prole might be absorbed into the entrepeneurial, managerial, or more infrequently of late, pop worlds.

There's little point in listing what happens in this song, the now-familiar story of the student blessed with inherited wealth who declares her intention of slumming it, and the bitter response this elicits – quite rightly, it's by far the group's most famous record, and parts of it have passed into the language. Attention needs to be drawn, though, to just how strange it is, how little it conforms to the classicist verse-chorus-verse structures so avidly fetishised by Britpop. Without ever falling into the direct parody occasionally indulged in at the time, it's a record completely formed by the 'motorik' of the early 1970s German groups Neu!, Harmonia and La Düsseldorf, a metronomic two-chord drone without solos, without any deliberate dynamics, changes of pace, 'middle eights' or the like, gaining its momentum through relentless, driving repetition. At the Reading Festival in 2000, Pulp underscored this by beginning their set with a monumental, shimmering drone which pulsated for some minutes before the first line was read and the audience realised they were listening to 'Common People'. Unlike the heavily structured melodrama of a 'Razzmatazz' or a 'Disco 2000' it doesn't sound remotely like an attempt to write a pop single, but the result, as with 'Inside Susan' or 'Sheffield: Sex City' of a drone and a monologue. In the context of the pop charts, it sounded deeply *un*common, exotic and unusual, conforming to no obvious pattern. The same can be said of the vocal, as what sounds at first like a piece of almost stand-up-comedy storytelling escalates into a scream of unadulterated rage.

You can hear this in the way that, at first, the lyric is full of mannerisms, the oft quoted 'I'll see what I can do' or the whispered 'are you sure...?', but four minutes later, the words are enunciated with a barely-controlled fury, what sounds like something pent-up for over a decade suddenly spilling over; certainly, you can't imagine that any of this was said at the time the question was asked. The song's most savage verse begins with a series of threats, where the 'common people' are imagined as 'a dog lying in the corner...it will bite you, and never warn you, look out...they'll tear your insides out...cause everybody hates a tourist...especially one who thinks it's all such a laugh'. The motorik-build up suddenly explodes, and he yells, palpably shaking with rage 'you will NEVER understand - how it FEELS to live your life - with no MEANING or CONTROL...you are AMAZED that they exist - and they burn so bright whilst you can only wonder why'. It's this outburst which is the centrepiece of 'Common People', and radio programmers obviously thought it a step too far, snipping it from most daytime edits. Here, there's both the reminder that what now seems like a subdued, depressed mass is quite capable of showing its teeth, and that class isn't a matter of 'smoking fags and playing pool', but of something much more fundamental – the lack of control over one's own life, the knowledge that you're condemned to be little more than a surplus, that there is no way out, no way that you could 'call your Dad and he'd stop it'. No exit.

What is it to be *common*, here? Partly it's where you live, miserable circumstances – flats above shops, crap jobs, the need to 'pretend you never went to school' in order to not be suspected of ideas above the station; but it's obvious that the word itself would only be spoken by someone who is not common. This was at a time in which proleing it up was *de rigeur*, from Blair's estuary vowels and glottal stops down to Blur's wholesale use of proleface. It's clear enough from *The Last Party* that 'Common People', irrespective of its beginnings in conversations with Greek sculpture students in the late 1980s, was to a large degree aimed at the group's apparent compatriots in Britpop, and particularly in Blur, whose frontman had become the most conspicuous example of the genre's class tourism, suddenly acquiring in 1993-

4 a previously unheard cockney accent and an interest in birds, football and suchlike. It's a minor shame that it gets written into another tale of sexual climbing, although after the early 'you want to sleep with common people like me', the boasting is abandoned (biographically, Jarvis Cocker admitted that this part of the story was untrue anyway). Here, at least, we could fairly say it's not 'a case of woman v man' - it's really directed at the nasal sneering at working class hedonism in 'Girls & Boys', at the idle 'social observation' doggerel of 'Parklife'.

Pulp might have seemed the refusenik 'neither Washington nor Moscow' option in the 'Country House'/'Roll With It' farrago, but that final clause in 'Common People' sounds closer to Blur's rivals; to the declarations of class pride that could be found in the odd early Oasis record, the snarled 'you're the outcast, you're the underclass, but you don't care, cos you're living fast' in 'Bring It On Down' - that, no matter how circumscribed, how hopeless your existence, its narrowness means that you experience things more intensely, a view that has its analogue in the gap year tourist's assertion that over there, they *really know how to live*. You are amazed that they exist. But to 'burn' here is not the 'shining' that always seems to occur in Oasis songs - it has the necessary concomitant that you'll burn out, that you will, eventually, be defeated. But in 'Common People' there's also a hint that Pulp and those they spoke for were not 'common' by choice, and Oasis' blithe 'but you don't care' is inconceivable. Class-consciousness is often sharpest at the margins, where it meets other classes, where it's aware of other options - where it is in some proximity to the enemy. In an environment where one class is all you know, it isn't so acute, and you can't maintain so much of an anger against a vaguely defined 'them' - as was amply demonstrated by Oasis' post-1995 embrace of the most hoary aspirational clichés. For Pulp and their constituency, you can tell that to 'pretend you never went to school' was every bit a strain as it might have been to those who were slumming it – more so, because it is forced upon you.

'Common People' is one of the most breathtaking moments of entryism in popular music, the moment of truth in Britpop's 'we've taken over!' lie. It also had the obvious effect of making sure the song could no longer be autobiographical. In terms of Pulp's music, it made them attempt the same anthemic-motorik-epic trick several times, some of which were more successful than others; it also tethered them for the next three years to the production services of Chris Thomas, chosen on the basis of the Wall Of Sound he'd erected on Roxy Music's *For Your Pleasure* and *Never Mind the Bollocks, Here's the Sex Pistols*. On 'Common People', his bludgeoning approach is absolutely perfect, and the arrangement, from the flickers of treated violin to the chattering synths that dominate, builds on exactly the things that made Pulp's sound distinctive in the first place, the things that made *NME* or *Q* journalists who were happier listening to Pavement reach for epithets like 'kitsch' or 'so bad it's good' – but soon, these alien elements – the ageing synthesisers, the creepily Slavic violin – were sidelined by guitars and significance-signifying orchestras, to mixed effect.

Though there is much in the song that, for all its familiarity, cannot be reduced to cliché, it did provide a series of aural tics and visual cues that could be easily remembered, parodied and made inoffensive. Amongst other things, 'Common People' needs to be considered in isolation as much as possible from its fairly awful video, a form Pulp had previously been much more imaginative with (and would be again later). Here, the common people are symbolised by what looks like the clientèle of a Camden indie disco, the club and the clothes all in the distinctively '90s saturated-colour version of the '70s; the dead-end dancing, drinking and screwing is personified in ironic dancing and ironic fighting, and at the centre of it are two, in the parlance, 'iconic' images; one, of a shrunken Jarvis carted round in a supermarket trolley by actress Sadie Frost, who was perhaps a prescient choice given her role in the gossip-column aristocracy of the 'Primrose Hill set'. Then, there's a tracking shot across a row of terraced-houses, all of them with cute little details, window baskets or right-to-buyed up windows, where the common or garden indie kids act out scenes of proletarian life on loop. It immediately evokes the very similar set of 'Parklife''s video a year earlier, and it's difficult to find any satirical intent in the borrowing; the saturated, ironic aesthetic is not terribly far either from Damien Hirst's unforgivable video to 'Country House' soon after. It's one of the only times where Pulp genuinely did look like the nudge-wink *Carry-On* sex comedy that the unobservant thought they always were; at least if you put your hands over your ears. The video's unthreatening cheerfulness might well have helped with the entryist labour of bringing the song to #1 in the pop charts, but in the process it fixed their image in a markedly reduced fashion.

We live round here too (oh really?)

All these contradictions are brought to the fore in the follow-up, 'Mis-Shapes', where the relentless momentum of 'Common People' takes on a newly insurgent tone. If Pulp's mid-90s records are best understood as a South Yorkshire retooling of disco, then 'Mis-Shapes' is their 'Ain't No Stoppin' Us Now'. As a statement of triumphant collectivity against the odds, it bottles the giddy feeling' that 'we' were on the move that accompanied both Britpop and early Blairism., and the knowledge of what false dawns both were is bound to colour any listening today. Not incidentally, it's a song the group themselves quickly grew to hate, and they didn't play it again from 1996 onwards, although they made a couple of curious attempts to rewrite it. The motorik pulse is replaced by a peculiarly prancing, piano-driven glam-stomp, and like those sleevenote communiques, it's addressed at the Pulp People, at the constituency of outcasts they acquired after 1992. We're defined by being poor, weird misshapen waste products, 'raised on a diet of broken biscuits', so when facing the enemy, we have to use 'the one thing we've got more of – that's our minds'; but we're also defined by certain choices – 'we don't look the same as you, we don't do the things you do', 'we weren't supposed to be, we learnt too much at school'. If it ended there, then that would be one thing – but other, grander associations are courted.

What makes 'Mis-Shapes' so exciting, other than the feeling – lesser than in 'Common People', but still electric – of someone finally finding the right words to convey an age-old grievance – is the way it speaks unashamedly in the language of class war, with the threat aimed directly at property: 'we want your *homes*, we want your *lives*, we want the *things you won't allow us*'; you hear someone who has unexpectedly chanced their way into the unexpected position of spokesman, and seizing the role with alacrity – or rather, using it as the way of avenging the defeats of the past, that hissed 'you think that you've got us beat, but revenge is going to be so sweet' – and there's nothing else produced by Britpop which takes on so fully the role of punk-style upending of received values. Yet though it might present itself as being about class conflict, 'Mis-Shapes' encapsulates rather more a conflict which anyone who went to a compre-hensive school or lived in a provincial town in the 1990s will be all too familiar with. That is, the one-sided fights between conformist, violent, sportswear-clad 'townies' and 'hippies'/'moshers'/'goths'/'indies' (otherwise competing tribes pushed into uneasy alliance by a shared and deeply relative nonconformism), fought out in corridors and precincts across the UK.

The phrase 'townie' itself – which Pulp used in interviews to describe 'Mis-Shapes'' adversaries - comes from the town vs gown conflicts of University cities. It's the students' derisive term for the inhabitants of the city that they're exploiting (or, more recently, that is exploiting them). It's also used by the teenagers that most probably will soon *be* students as a counter-insult to the usual 'poof', 'dyke' and suchlike directed at anyone who doesn't quite fit. So it's deeply double-edged. In the context of school, or at a weekend in the centre of town, it's an expression of weakness, a word you direct at those who directly act to make your life a misery; but by the time you're at university, it expresses a far loftier contempt. In that, for anyone who, like the present author, got given a black eye in the centre of town for wearing a 'Mis-Shapes' T-shirt, the song still elicits an intense feeling of belonging. Here is a record that appeared to dramatise our daily predicament in the plainest of terms.

In class terms, though, it hardly mapped onto 'haves against haven'ts'. In the mid-90s, judging at least on personal experience, most (if not all) 'townies' were more-or-less working class, raised in an environment which is much more apt to violently enforce conformity, the duress of everyday life causing an all-too-often suspicious attitude to 'difference', towards getting funny ideas. Meanwhile, most (if not all) of 'us' were either middle class or raised at the intersection where the self-educated working class meets the bohemian lower-middle, where reading books were not something to be ashamed of (i.e, with backgrounds like Pulp themselves), and oh, how all of us loved 'Mis-Shapes'! - even the Green Day fans, so perfectly did it describe our literally embattled position. But why are those who torture the 'Mis-Shapes' every weekend so inclined to play the lottery when they're in so much more privileged a position than their prey? You can hear why Pulp were later so embarrassed by 'Mis-Shapes' when it reaches quasi-Albarn sneers like 'what's the point in being rich, when you can't think what to do with it – 'cause you're so bleeding *thick*'.

What 'Mis-Shapes' does beautifully – and, irrespective of the group's own disdain, this is a thrilling, totally convincing pop single, one of their best - is lay claim to working-class intelligence against the notion of class as mere identity and ethnicity, sportswear and accents, thuggery and racism. Instead it says we, 'coming out of the sidelines', are the true misfits, those who won't fit either into the tastefully arranged world of the middle-classes or the enforced stupidity of a defeated proletariat. It's enormously exciting as an idea, a call to arms where we will rise up and take over from M People on one side and Oasis on the other, and it's hard not be carried away with its insurgent pride in awkwardness. But it's a fantasy, however wonderful that fantasy might be. We're wrenched out of class-as-essentialism, but where to? A solidarity of clothes and records, of freely-chosen identities as indie kids in charity shop threads?

Pedro Romhanyi's video dramatises it in terms as horribly dated and Britpop-ridden as his video to 'Common People', although this one is significantly funnier. We're in a nightclub again, where a townies vs 'us' fight is brewing; 'we' again look like the members of Menswear and Cast, while 'they' are casuals. Yet of a weirdly dated sort – rather than the Ben Sherman shirts and Puffa jackets of the genuine mid-90s thug, they're dressed as the likely late-70s tormentors of Pulp themselves, dressed in Fred Perrys, skinny ties, short skirts, sequins and wedges. 15 years later, it's all completely reversed, as the vintage tracksuit jackets and overgrown Liam Gallagher shagcuts worn by 'us' in the video are much more likely to be the uniform of someone kicking your head in outside Wetherspoons, while the circa-1980 thug-wear worn by 'them' fits perfectly with the never-ending 1980s revival favoured by vaguely bohemian or indie youth. What saves the video is the fact that Jarvis Cocker plays the leader of both gangs, once as 'himself' in brown velvet jacket, once as the evil angry prole alterego in skinny tie and pencil moustache. It's a welcome pointer that the divide is not nearly as clear as the song – and us – wanted it to be. The them and us in 'Mis-Shapes' is wishful thinking, an urge to take the moral force of class warfare and apply it to a rather less righteous fight between the wearers of different jackets. Any real battle between haves and haven'ts would involve some common cause between bullied, intellectual dole youth such as Pulp once were, and the lads and ladies who chased them around town every Saturday. The song still carries, though, the urge to reimagine the divides of class, to produce some sort of alternative collectivity. As a single, it was double-A-side with a song which remembered another moment of failed communalism, a genuine and brief attempt to live in common – rave.

It didn't mean Nothing

The intensity of rave's effect on Pulp is easily garnered from 'Sorted for E's and Wizz', where an affectionate remembrance is very quickly followed by a disappointed, even embittered rejection. Its peculiar amalgam of campfire singalong and ghostly rave keyboard hooks starts off with anticipation, making all the arrangements for a rave somewhere in the vicinity of the M25, in some obscure field in the London green belt – getting the drugs together, getting the tickets 'off some fucked up bloke in Camden Town' (a rare mention in their songs for the capital of Britpop, notably in a non-indie context), and trying hardly successfully to work out from pirate radio where the field in question is. At first the mordant tone can't quite hide the excitement, the 'tell me when the spaceship lands, cos all this has just got to mean something' isn't wholly a joke, and there's a thrill as much as fear in knowing that 'at 4 o'clock the normal world seems very, very far away' - but after that, it's just another load of unfulfilled promises. The rest of the song is yelped negations and terrors, caused more than anything else by just how much it originally promised, a total repudiation of the obsessive private worlds investigated in *His 'N' Hers*, a release from a class-bound environment, even from the self – 'everybody asks your name, they say we're all the same!' - only to find in their place another kind of vacant, grinning idiocy that's, if anything, even worse. 'Now it's nice one, geezer, and that's as far as the conversation went' implies that a couple of hours ago, when the pills where still working, the conversation could have been reaching elsewhere.

We end with sheer terror both of loss-of-self and of being stuck in the godforsaken M25 hinterland; in his most Alan Bennett voice, he wishes he could call his mother. In an optimistic reading, Simon Reynolds considered the 'Sorted' sleevenote – 'The summer of 89. Centreforce FM, Santa Pod, Sunrise 5000, "Ecstacy Airport", ride the white horse, the strings of life, dancing at motorway service stations, falling asleep at the wheel on the way home. There's so many people - it's got to mean something, it needs to mean something, surely it must mean something. IT DIDN'T MEAN NOTHING' – to have a double meaning, holding on at least partly to this disappeared moment of collectivism, which the record maybe shares, in its enduring warmth and wit, its evident affection for another lost utopia. That's as maybe. What is true is that the more anarchic communal utopia of rave was largely supplanted by the superclub (indoors) and the music festival or large-scale 'event' concert (outdoors). Pulp specialised in the latter, with Jarvis Cocker developing a rambling, occasionally vaguely messianic stand-up routine for these occasions, which were somewhere between rave's pop-up instant cities and the completely circumscribed world of stadium rock. It didn't mean that much either.

Certainly, the very attempt to speak frankly about rave's pleasures and pitfalls in 'Sorted for Es and Wizz' meant that the song was practically banned, with its more conventionally Britpoppy double-A-side usually played instead; when on telly or on the radio, the title had to be shortened to 'Sorted'. The same year, that phrase appeared on posters all over the country with the face of Leah Betts, one of Ecstasy's rare fatalities. Pulp's designers, by this point with Blue Source replacing the Designers

Republic, played on its title by creating a make-your-own speed wrap kit, leading to sudden tabloid notoriety; in a seeming retro gesture back to their 'The Filth and the Fury' headline for the Sex Pistols, the sleeve made the front page of the Daily Mirror as BAN THIS SICK STUNT. From now, and for the next two or three years, Pulp were officially pop stars and official tabloid heroes/villains, subject to everything from kiss and tell stories to a 'Justice for Jarvis' campaign accompanying the Michael Jackson incident. Any attempt to say anything remotely complex would immediately be subsumed in tabloid hysteria, which makes it especially intriguing how easily Pulp managed to disappear three years later.

The right to be different, that's all

In *Different Class* you can hear Pulp at their insurgent peak, finally reaching – and clearly massively enjoying – the instruments of mass communication, using much of the record as a means of expressing in the most palatable and radio-playable form some deeply unpalatable truths. You can also hear a conformism beginning, tentatively, to overpower them. The lyrics are starting to lose, perhaps deliberately, their previous extreme specificity and their obsessive layers of detail, instead following 'Common People' towards a new universalism, an attempt to communicate as directly as possible, without wanting to scare anyone off with outré mentions of pink quilted eiderdowns, penetrating pavements or sky-blue trainer bras. This works best the more there is something of note to communicate. The singles, 'Monday Morning' and especially the astonishing, far less on-message 'I Spy' are the sound of the bitterest of resentments forming themselves into coherent expression; 'Underwear' and 'Live Bed Show' take the feverish sexual obsessions of earlier records and strip out most of the '70s signifiers and the more outrageous non-verbal utterances, to convincing effect, with anything more perverse kept under control; 'F.E.E.L.I.N.G.C.A.L.L.E.D.L.O.V.E' and the spectacularly seedy *His 'N' Hers* remnant 'Pencil Skirt' smuggle some of it back in.

The record presents itself both as fun-for-all-the-family and communique from 'out of the sidelines', a particularly unstable combination; the sleevenote message this time isn't so much directed at the troops but at those who might be less sympathetic. 'Please understand...we just want the right to be different'. That insistence on the importance of 'difference', that anyone at an art school in the late '80s will have encountered in a more recondite form, the particular as a counter to the claims of universalism and grand narratives, is equally unstable – the record finds them wanting to maintain their otherness and making an entirely successful bid at co-hosting *The Big Breakfast* and getting their faces on the covers of the tabloids. Blue Source's cover concept takes this literally to an enduringly surreal level, by photographing a group of cut-outs in various locations, appearing usually as unearthly, monochrome voyeurs, out of place wherever they stood, whether looking over courting teenagers and a couple humping on a heath, stood in a desolate exurban car park or about to enter a bedroom with a woman waiting inside in her underwear, or sat enjoying tea and a Mondrian mosaic in Luigi's Café, Clerkenwell. It's a great sleeve, but again dulled by familiarity - one of the cut-out Jarvises later provided part of the set for the deeply unlovely Britpop telly staple *TFI Friday*.

The slightly unsatisfying nature of *Different Class* lies where the class-and-sex focus slips and a nascent classicism takes over, especially on the homily of 'Something Changed' and the closing 'Bar Italia'. The former sounds like he'd decided to rewrite *It* with his relatively newfound lyrical gifts, a Bacharachian, strings-and-acoustics attempt to write a classic Our Tune, not without charm, but setting what would be a worrying precedent on the next two records and especially on his solo albums and side-projects, towards an embrace of the eternal heroic clichés of romantic love and classic MOR songwriting. It's especially dispiriting to find someone who had previously written love songs that included what 'Someone Like the Moon' called 'all the mess' writing something so cutesy; perhaps he needed a break from seediness and menace. 'Bar Italia' meanwhile is a fun, battered and drunken singalong that plods the album to a close more than a little disappointingly. These attempts to write something reasonably straight suggest that Jarvis was already starting to tire of his vengefully lubricious *metier*. A well might have been starting to dry up.

So just lie against the wall, watch my conscience disappear

When Pulp's Island albums were belatedly re-released, each with an extra CD of B-sides and outtakes, those for *His 'N' Hers* and *This Is Hardcore* were, as much as *The World Won't Listen* and *Hatful of Hollow*, good enough to stand on their own; the extras for *Hardcore* were arguably better than the original album itself. The pickings for *Different Class* were nothing like as rich. There's 'Mile End' and 'Catcliffe Shakedown', both of which seem much more of a piece with *His 'N' Hers;* or there's the innuendo-laden froth of 'Paula' and 'Parent Teacher Association', the former being easily the most straightforwardly, guiltlessly sexist thing Jarvis Cocker ever wrote, wisely left unreleased at the time, but saved on record by a hilariously inept guitar solo from Russell Senior (a derisive reference, maybe, to their increasing spin towards proper rock music?). Its subject matter – you're dead stupid, but I don't half fancy you – would become lyrical conceit of choice for the Arctic Monkeys' Alex Turner. These come along with a couple of failed attempts at writing big pop singles, like the throwaway 'Ansaphone' and the sub-'Mis-Shapes' we're-on-the-move anthem 'We Can Dance Again' - and not much else. One of the more telling moments is in the nondescript 'Don't

Lose It', where Cocker's self-awareness is starting to fade into self-hatred, the deceptively third-person song sounding like a warning to a woman that if she sleeps with him, he'll use her as subject matter – 'don't lose it – he wants to use it, and put it in a song to sing'. There would be a lot more of this soon. And throughout, the less straight elements of Pulp's sound, the synths, the violin, the heavy-breathing and monologues, are gradually being streamlined into something resembling a rock band.

This is all minor carping. For the most part, *Different Class* is their *The Queen Is Dead*, the gleeful seizure of a momentary power over the nation's adolescents. At times, the new universalism to the lyrics is striking in its directness. The Tindersticks-like 'Live Bed Show', a grandiose funeral march for a sexual relationship soured, focuses again on interiors, this time centring on one object – a bed purchased for ten pounds, 'from a shop just down the road' seven years previously. The horror of domesticity is personified in a woman trying unsuccessfully to convince herself that the good times aren't over, and while the man barely exists, the song comes across as being equally sympathetic and fatalistic. While a '59 Lyndhurst Grove' blames external factors for erotic boredom – ie, suggests that she needs a real, northern man rather than some poncey London architect – this one blames nobody, seeing instead something as inevitable and miserable as the ageing process. It's a terribly sad record, the grandeur of its arrangement a cruel joke. The final knife, that 'if this show was televised, no-one would watch it' brings some of the voyeurism back – as does, in spades, 'Pencil Skirt', a hysterically-charged re-run of 'Acrylic Afternoons', taking the Sheffield Casanova persona to absurd proportions ('I've kissed your mother twice, and now I'm working on your Dad'), over a backing alternately sleazily elegant and furtively muffled. At its climax, our hero is finally confronted, and offers a series of yelped excuses – we realise that sex is not about sex, not some act valuable for its own sake. 'I only come here, 'cos I know it makes you sad; I only do it, cause I know you know it's bad – oh don't you know it's ugly, and it shouldn't be like that, oh but – *it's turning me on'*. It's a remarkable outburst, a sudden confession of his own venality, that he can only even be excited by the prospect of revenge, capture or power. In its way, this is a vision of human relationships far bleaker than anything on *Freaks*, with the dry humour ('if you can look under the bed, you can see my house from here') the sneakiest of entryist alibis.

Some of Britpop's inspirations plumped for the more avant-garde of the mid-90s' musical movements. David Bowie in particular faced corrosive music press ridicule for calling in A Guy Called Gerald to produce him when he could have opted for Stephen Street. 'F.E.E.L.I.N.G.C.A.L.L.E.D.L.O.V.E', along with 'I Spy' the album's singular masterwork, marks the only notable example of anyone directly associated with Britpop listening to jungle at its height and incorporating a few of its ideas – although in this as ever they were shadowed by Noel Gallagher, who played guitar on Goldie's atrocious metal-drum&bass mess 'Temper Temper' a few years later. Here, Candida Doyle and Russell Senior, at least assuming that they're respectively playing the various synths and unnervingly treated violins here, create the last, and one of the finest of their spacious electronic landscapes, backing the last until 2001 of Jarvis Cocker's spoken-word monologues; his intonations are punctuated by sudden little jungle fusillades, which escalate into the mildest of timestretched breaks in the melodramatic chorus. And melodrama this is, because this time, in line with the new perversions-for-the-millions line, rather than speaking of bus journeys in Sheffield or shabby cuckoldings in the suburbs, we are being regaled with the story of love itself, its destructive power and inscrutability. Yet the universal is not a nice place. The emptiness, the seamy electronics, the outbreaks of junglist clatter, create what sounds like the coldest of environments, taken somewhere quite different from the warmly shabby Sheffield of old, but into somewhere identikit, alienating – 'the same events shuffled in a slightly different order each day, just like a modern shopping centre', and rather than the allure of specificity, of individuality and joyous crankiness that animates *Intro*, this is the sex appeal of the inorganic in its coldest form, something which would soon lead the lyricist into the particularly inhuman world of hardcore pornography.

My Favourite Parks

For a band so often accused of nostalgia, there are – the wonderful and completely flimsy, almost self-parodic 'Disco 2000' aside – few warm memories of the past in this record. Nostalgic is a word too often applied to anything centred on memory, no matter how complex or bitter that might be; and *Different Class'* two main essays in memory are hardly the matter of fond reminisce. 'Monday Morning''s uncharacteristically angular post-punk, though probably to blame for Franz Ferdinand, is a frantic dramatisation of failed escape, pulled between the inertia of the dole wastrel – 'why live in the world, when you can live in your head' – and the compulsory hedonism of the 1990s, seeing both as dead-ends, and demanding instead that 'the past must die for the future to be born', but Pulp, unlike the jungle producers they were borrowing the odd idea from, were unable to take that futurist leap; and so the inertia continues. Instead, a direct confrontation with the past is narrated through their most delirious, most vicious and vindictive revenge fantasy, which by now was quite clearly a revenge actuality.

'I Spy' is where the mask is torn off, where the genial, Alan Bennett-via-Bryan Ferry pop star with his funny lyrics about sex and common folk and his funny little dance, truly reveals himself. It's not pretty, but – especially for those of us who have more or less guilty sympathies with it – it's a breathtaking, thrilling affair, where our hero places himself in exactly the role all of us had fantasised about, where he does what we were all dreaming of – an act of the pettiest revenge committed with the most righteous of motivations. It begins in the 'worst place in the world', which could so easily be a sleeping bag in a disused factory in the rotting post-industrial expanses of Sheffield, a collapsing, asbestos fibred system-built flat in Mile End, or the listener could fill in their own example. A cinematic, John Barry theme for strings and tremulous guitars flutters around a coldly enunciated whisper, voyeuristic and accusative – 'oh, you didn't do bad – you made it out. I'm still stuck here...oh but I'll get out...oh yeah, I'll *get out.*'

The dance begins, an orchestral disco where the big budget and the overstuffed production Chris Thomas brought to Pulp is at its most opulent, a parodic dance of increasingly monstrous malice. First, we're still in the realms of fantasy, the figure dumped miserably on the dole insisting on his grandiose plans, what seem like ludicrous self-assertions. 'It may look to the untrained eye I'm sitting on my arse all day – I'm biding time, until I take you on', and we realise exactly why this isn't an idle threat but something resembling a military operation – 'I've got your number, taken notes, I know the way your minds work, I have *studied'*. And what he has studied is the frieze of self-protection, the impeccable, unruffled self-assurance of the bourgeois, realising just how little actually separates them and him other than mere privilege and character armour – the voice yelps up several octaves at 'and your minds are just the same as mine, except that you're all clever swine – you never let the mask slip, you never admit to it – you're never hurried'. The plan reveals itself to be the destruction of the life of two, seemingly randomly chosen members of this privileged class, honed to precision every night (and in this, it's extremely hard not to see some heavy autobiography in the song, in the countless years signing on and fruitlessly toiling) - 'I will blow your paradise away'. It's this singular nature that makes 'I Spy' such a grotesque tragedy, the fact that once there might have been the prospect of some kind of collective advancement, a way out together, a way of destroying not just one fairly unimportant couple's life but of making sure they never need to exist. 'I Spy' is the sound of class war as desperate individual acts of terrorism – and it exudes a similar sense of righteous anti-social glee as the sight of Charles and Camilla's limousine being assaulted. *You are not safe.*

At this point, the song swerves into straight-faced ludicrousness, with the class-war Casanova's unmasking leading to confessions that sound like Alexander Herzen's diary rewritten by Adrian Mole, where the megalomaniac, egomaniac grossness of the fantasy becomes clear. This part, at least, is probably *supposed* to be funny, although it's as horribly believable as all the rest. As the metronomic pulse subsides and a pounding orchestra replaces it, he gasps 'oh, it's just like in the old days – I used to compose my own critical notices in my head.' There's a real audience here, this time, you see. 'The crowd gasp at Cocker's masterful control of the bicycle...imagining a blue plaque over the place I ever touched a girl's chest'. Then we get to the plan for their destruction and it is, of course, revenge through sex, directed at the man in the couple we spy in the introduction. 'You see you should take me seriously. Very seriously indeed. Because I've been sleeping with your wife for the past sixteen weeks. Smoking your cigarettes. Drinking your brandy...you see I spy for a living, and I specialise in revenge. I'm taking the things' – cue choir - 'I know will cause you pain'. And why? 'I can't help it', he mutters, and you can hear him grinning, 'I was dragged up....'

What of the woman in this couple, whose life is being torn apart with such glee? Well, her very privilege itself makes her sexier, makes her all the more desirable – the irresistible smell of money. The strings spiral upwards, the dance starts again, with the cry 'your Ladbroke Grove looks turn me on!', before proceeding to itemise everything from her dress to the 'milliont-housands of tiny dryness lines' of her face, adding the promise that 'I will take you from this sickness, dinner parties and champagne...I'll hold your body, and make it sing again'. So all this could easily be subsumed into kitchen sink cinema's tales of revenge-through-sexual-conquest, be put alongside Lawrence Harvey's malevolent Bradfordian in *Room at the Top* – but it's nastier, more precise and more conscious than all that; and there's no hint of Mellors teaching Lady Chatterley about the innocent joys of base pleasures here. The sex is mediated, it's the means to an end, and the woman is every bit the victim here as her husband – more so. It ends, almost disconsolately, at the beginning, with the fantasist spying his prey - 'I spy a chance, to change the world', he trills, and then realises what a lie that actually is, and settles instead for the act of individual, partial but briefly oh-so-satisfying destruction – 'to change *your* world'. As if nothing more than that was possible. On the album, 'I Spy' follows 'Common People', and it seems far from accidental. The first could be seen as charting the attainment of class consciousness, the realisation of the class war's existence - and the second the avenging response to that revelation, a doomed guerilla action in belated retaliation.

As a measure of how far Pulp had come, now even this was supposed to be palatable TV fare. After they'd finished touring *Different Class*, Pulp did not, to my knowledge, ever play 'I Spy' again – one suspects it gave away too much, was embarrassingly self-revealing of either Jarvis Cocker's fantasies or, quite possibly according to the gossip columns of the time, how he was actually living his life in 1995. In that year, in the midst of one of *Later...With Jools Holland*'s boogie-woogie/indie/acid jazz horrors, Pulp played their new single and one from the album, which was of course 'I Spy' (what else?). Sensing that they were now, more surely than at any other point, in the smuggest of enemy territory – far more so than when on *Top of the Pops* – they gave easily the most memorable performance ever seen on that show, where the revenge-crazed character is played with total, unforgettable conviction. What on earth could people have made of this? What did they think was going on? Like with much else, you can read in most articles on Pulp a refusal to even think about it, to subsume it instead under general 'perviness' in order to remain untroubled. Or, more likely, one ex-prole was now allowed to think he'd won, for a little while.

If this show was televised, no-one would watch it...

For the next year, Pulp now acted as if their fame was an instrument, trying to become the ideal pop stars, behaving in exactly the manner they'd been planning for so long, willingly throwing themselves into every TV show and every music festival, with their frontman developing a less heroic liking for compulsive ligging, by all accounts. Some of these performances are enshrined in Britpop legend – replacing the Stone Roses as headliners of the Glastonbury Festival in 1995, playing 'Sorted for Es and Wizz' for the first time in its most appropriate setting (or at least it was, after the demise of the orbital rave) and regaling the crowd with various raconteur turns, acting an increasingly both convincing and silly role as leader of the insurgent youth.

I saw Pulp play for the first time at the start of 1996, travelling to London, driven by a friend's Dad up to Owen Williams' massive, shabby hangar, Wembley Arena. We felt horribly young and horribly uncool, unable to afford the mock-second-hand threads that everyone was dressed in – felt fairly freakish, in fact, compared with all these beautiful people. The performance itself was weirdly unmemorable, something we watched from a far distance on video screens rather than through watching the little man on the stage. Pulp by this point were as distant as any stadium rock act, a speck far, far away in the stratosphere; yet at the same time they were constantly in your living room. Included among the marvellous cabinet of curiosities on Pulp's 2002 *Hits* DVD is a short film called *TV Madness*, reformed out of clips taken from their innumerable television appearances between 1995 and 1998; the group members participate in a fashion parade, they sit around the table with Gaby Roslin at 8am for *The Big Breakfast*, and answer questions about pets for *Live and Kicking*. It's a mind-boggling film, a videodrome of awe-inspiring inanity, with our protagonists looking defeated and baffled as often as they're seizing the opportunity. In one clip from an Italian television show, a young woman declares (in Italian) her passionate and unending love for Jarvis Cocker with such prolix and physical intensity that she looks on the verge of bursting into tears; the presenter/interpreter tells the singer that she wants to make him quiche. Then there's the parodies and tributes that come with that level of fame.such as Jonathan Ross introducing a truly horrible supper-club version of 'Common People' or. Blouse and their (absolutely pitch-perfect) Pulp parody 'Oh Myra', courtesy of *Brass Eye*.

The wager with Pulp's fifteen minutes of fame was pure substitutionism - they were supposed to be doing what we'd all wanted to do, they were supposed to be our surrogates, there in the heart of the reality studio, sabotaging it as we'd all like to think we would. If *TV Madness* shows, on the contrary, their complete lack of control, then what of The Michael Jackson Incident? For the few who don't know, this occurred at the Brit Awards in early 1996 not very long after Jarvis Cocker was lifted from the ground to strike a Christ-like pose at the end of Pulp's performance of 'Sorted for Es and Wizz'. Michael Jackson, in town for a Lifetime Achievement award, then at the height of his madness and fresh from some bought-off accusations of institu-tionalised pederasty in Neverland, was performing 'Earth Song', in which he saves the world from sundry ecological threats. On the stage, he was surrounded with children of all conceivable races, who are saved from the catastrophe under his embrace. At a climactic point, Cocker ran onto the stage, bent over, made some derisive hand-movements and then scuttled off. It happened in a matter of seconds, and none of us watching actually noticed it – it had to be picked out later on during the news, because Jarvis Cocker had been arrested, and spent a night in the cells under suspicion, amusingly enough, of assaulting some of the children, though he was exonerated almost as quickly.

So he'd done what 'we' all wished we could do at a ceremony as ridiculous and self-important as the Brit Awards, and moreover he'd done so at the most ridiculous and self-important moment imaginable; moreover, at a particularly horrendous example of hypocrisy, indulged in by the untouchable pop aristocracy, by the pop despot who had floated neo-Stalinist statues of himself up the Thames a few months earlier. Yet in a sense this too was another of the mid-90s' pyrrhic victories. The pop lineage which ends with Pulp was based unashamedly on the declaration 'ridicule is nothing to be scared of', and rather than rushing the stage during, say, Oasis, or Blur, or U2 or someone similarly tedious (but who they would be more likely to bump into at parties), instead all the derision was aimed at one of the last genuine freaks left, at someone whose self-creation had reached an extent a Bowie (or a Jarvis Cocker) couldn't even have dreamed about – into an extraordinary being neither perceptibly male or female, black or white, asexual and alien. He might have been waving his arse at the ludicrous spectacle erected by a suspected paedophile with dictatorial pretensions, by all means – but such a protest could easily be embraced as an ordinary lad from Sheffield getting in there and having a go at the weirdos. From the mid-1990s onwards, from the 'realness'-obsessed world of gangsta to the self-effacing ordinary (and more-and-more-frequently public school-)boys of British indie, pop stars had from henceforth to be ordinary blokes. Even at this vengeful peak, it's hard to say whether the mistakes and misfits were winning.

Not that there wasn't a venal jouissance in this, too. The last, valedictory moment of this particular phase wasn't on a Pulp record at all, but a track sung by Jarvis Cocker on Barry Adamson's *Oedipus Schmoedipus*, one of those very mid-90s 'soundtracks to an imaginary film' – probably the best of them, an album about sex, utopia and power highly analogous to Pulp's best work. The song, called 'Set The Controls For The Heart of the Pelvis', is an insight into fame psychosis, 'I Spy' megalomania with all the righteous anger replaced by salivating idiot desire, crashing along on a Sly Stone sample and a gospel chorus singing in unison the refrain 'save me from my own hand!' The lyric revels in new-found fame and power ('I enter a room and *all* the girls say - 'come on Jarv, can I be the first?'), throwing itself all the way into a series of instantly forgotten fucks – as an ethos we're in exactly the same mindset as something like Jay-Z's 'Big Pimpin', something that cold, that amoral and propulsive. Just offscreen is what he's recently left – 'don't leave me alone in this double-bed...it smells of damp towels and asthma inhalers...save my from my own hand, save me from my mother's life...save me'.

4

That Goes In There

What do you fear? Being found out. Then why do you always give yourself away? What do you want to do? Hide. Then why go out and make an exhibition of yourself? What do you seek? Oblivion.
The Fall, 'Arms Control Poseur' (1990)

Funny How It All Falls Away

After a tour in 1996, Pulp disappeared for what was considered an unseemly length of time. Rumours circulated, and still do, of all the rockbiz rockstar-in-decline clichés being fulfilled in spades, one by one - heroin addiction, depression, 'nervous exhaustion' and, in the departure of Russell Senior, 'musical differences'. Senior hadn't sung on a Pulp record since 'This House is Condemned', but since ten years previous he always seemed like the Eno to Jarvis' Bryan Ferry, a near-non-musician, a permanently staring, impressively attired presence at the side of the stage, politically and artistically erudite. Along with Candida Doyle's synthesisers, his violin atmospheres and elementary, but often peculiarly, queasily treated and always thoroughly non-rock guitar were the most interesting and unorthodox elements of Pulp's sound. He was quoted as saying he didn't think it was 'cool' to be in Pulp anymore. However, any Eno comparisons soon seemed extravagant when his post-Pulp career entailed producing a Serge Gainsbourg covers band, playing guitar in the short-lived post-Pulp glam act Venini, and setting up an antique shop. Nonetheless, something seemed to have gone awry with Pulp, now presented with the inescapable question, after the extreme ambiguity of their conquest, of what exactly to do with their achievements, of what they could smuggle in through their seemingly firm hold over a generation of adolescents' dreams and affections.

On the initial evidence of their comeback single, squeezing into the top ten near the end of 1997, they weren't particularly bothered. 'Help the Aged' sounded at first like an atypically melancholy *Different Class* outtake, choked into overproduced submission by Chris Thomas at his most bombastic, with a wearily predictable post-Britpop Anthemic Chorus of explosions, bells and whistles. It seemed at first as if they'd plumped for the option of playing it as safe as possible, though over time the song's qualities became more clear. 'Help the Aged' is notable for its unsentimental yet compassionate, self-implicating and deadly straight-faced stare at the onrush of ageing, loneliness and physical decline, all of which were no doubt weighing on the mind of its 33-year-old singer; and his precise, hushed, poignantly phrased delivery make it all the more so, Nonetheless, at the time, for anyone hoping for surprises, or for a public statement comparable to *Different Class'* spokesman-for-a-generation ambitions, it was deadly disappointing, the sound of a band trying unconvincingly to maintain that everything was ok.

Pulp, according closely with the lineage from which they came, were always a group whose aesthetics, sleeves, videos and clothes, were nearly as important, or as important, as their records. It was and is never 'all about the music'. So it's fitting that the real signs that something fundamental had changed with 'Help the Aged' were in Peter Saville's sleeve and Hammer & Tongs' video, wilfully embracing all the accusations of voyeurism and seediness. On the cover the group stand around in a hotel bedroom, with the singer, clad now and for the next few years in large, tinted glasses, peering through the blinds, looking every inch the malevolent figure of 'I Spy' and 'Set the Controls'. In the background, a painting by John Currin and an empty, made bed, the former depicting a very young woman and a 'distinguished' man. The sinister air was alloyed a little by the fact that the man looked like Noddy Holder.

The video, meanwhile, was by a long chalk their best since their self-directed efforts in 1992-3. Pop celebrity and one-word-name-icon Jarvis creeps through the video, spending much of it sat in a stairlift, refusing throughout to do his funny little dance, or to enact any other Jarvisian mannerisms; he and the group are dressed and shot as icily glamorous 1950s film stars, making the charity shop glam of 1994 seem gauche; the directors glaze the proceedings in an unearthly sheen, following the band and what looks like the guests at a particularly opulent dinner party through old age and eventually – of course – into the heavens, escaping physical limits into a concert in an interstellar dome, an extravagant fantasy to delay the inevitable. The B-sides, typically, supported suspicions that Pulp weren't settling on extending their allotted fifteen minutes. One was a rejected Bond theme retitled 'Tomorrow Never Lies', sung in a conspiratorial whisper rather than a smooth croon, pervaded with bloody and bleak images; the James Bond revival, the return of its once-unacceptable melange of absurd imperial nostalgia and coldly modern misogyny, was another consequence of Britpop/New Lad's restoration revaluations, but this unusable theme went straight for its empty heart. The other was 'Laughing Boy', an unexpected and beautifully disconsolate exercise in country balladry (with Casio), where the Sheffield Casanova is now cuckolded, plaintively asking 'who is this laughing boy, who ladders your tights? Could you tell him to cut the noise, 'cause it's spoiling my nights...' Meanwhile, by some way the most intriguing strictly *musical* thing Pulp did at this point was fill in for John Peel on Radio 1 for a week. I recorded one at the time, and it still stands as fantastic radio, a strange and wonderful mix of deadpan dialogues, absurdist competitions and fabulous music, with guitarist Mark Webber displaying especially outré tastes, and the rest introducing the unsuspecting to everything from Magazine to '50s exotica to DAF's 'Der Mussolini'.

In this unprepossessing single and the more promising ephemera around it, is encapsulated the final four years of Pulp's existence before they called their recently concluded indefinite hiatus. They would be caught between an impulse to embrace their sinister, uncomfortable side on the one hand, on the other to honour a contractual obligation to be enormously popular pop stars. In the process, they never quite created an album that really was the masterpiece they were capable of, nor did they manage to avoid a startlingly swift loss of any commercial standing. Nonetheless, the two albums that resulted are, in their way, more replete with peculiar corners and occasional monuments of unique, unrepeatable brilliance than the often over-smooth *Different Class*; both of them are the noblest of failures. Two albums that both sounded like endings, like two different ways out, one of them attempting (not always successfully) to be bitter, vengeful and *noir*, the other (not always successfully) trying to conclude with forgiveness, sweetness and light. In the process they created a couple of outright masterpieces, and it's to one of these that we must now turn, with some trepidation.

The End of the Line

To say 'This is Hardcore' was a shock after this tentative toe-dipping is something of an understatement. 'I Spy' was unnerving enough, but wrapped as it was in a flamboyant, danceable 'I Will Survive' arrangement, its unadulterated hatreds might have seemed palatable, or at least easily ignorable to the millions who heard it. 'This is Hardcore', where that flounce and panache is stripped away, has no such dressing. It's a fearful, genuinely horrifying record, the equal in its myopic, nihilistic worldview to anything produced by a Throbbing Gristle or an Oxbow, and equal in its total conviction to 'Common People's by now suddenly humanistic class warfare; a piece of musical and textual extremism which stands as the furthest any major, commercially-successful group in pop history had ever taken the pop single. It makes the at the time fairly controversial twists-and-turns of Radiohead's contemporary 'Paranoid Android' sound like callow public schoolboys playing at menace. Least of all does it bear comparison to other post-Britpop attempts to be 'difficult', say to Blur's swerve to alleged 'left-field' via skronky guitars and Pavement records.

It stands instead in the absolute first rank of the something-is-going-horribly-wrong-in-the-pop-charts genre, alongside Japan's 'Ghosts', Laurie Anderson's 'O Superman' or The Specials' 'Ghost Town'. Its relentlessly pessimistic worldview, its lack of any concession to humanity, compassion or the world outside a camera and two bodies, the terrible, wrenching drag of its arrangement, puts it at a point of no return even these were unable to reach. And while the above might have been capable of connecting their (geopolitical or personal) terrors with a wider public, the horror of 'This is Hardcore' is so intimate, so specific, that its commercial failure is easily understandable. Nobody would confess to having shared these thoughts, although within a few years many, many people would have undertaken the act it describes. It got to number 12 on its release at the start of 1998, and no subsequent Pulp single would chart higher. It's not an exaggeration to say that it stopped their career as pop stars stone dead – commercial suicide, for once, in the aid of a singular work of art rather than as a sloppy consequence of rock star petulance. One can only speculate about the efforts or ultimatums the group must have offered in order to convince Island to release it as a single. Its baleful effect was such that the album which shared its title has an entirely undeserved reputation as a work of similar power and conviction.

It is, to condense, a first-person story about amateur porn, the tale of a couple making their own hardcore film, putting the act on video and then then getting a sudden and exceptionally acute attack of post-coital *tristesse*. A deathly locked-groove somewhere between funeral march and the sleaziest funk crashes alongside a looped, smeared brass sample, and a Hammer Horror piano dolefully introduces the first verse. The voice is croaked, an Ian Curtis-like croon, murmuring of sex in the starkest, most mechanical terms. 'You are hardcore – you make me hard'. The seduction lines all sound tired, taken as much from the films as from anywhere else - 'I like your get up...I want it bad. I want it now' - but seemingly effective for that, as he assures his partner in this endeavour that she is the fulfilment of all his fantasies, all that he has ever wanted. 'It seems I saw you in some teenage wet dream', he enunciates in a lobotomised, obsessive drone. It soon becomes clear that she's not *really* the object of fantasy, here, but rather what could be done with her – the way that she could be mediated. 'I've *seen all the pictures*' and – recalling 'I Spy' here - 'I *studied them forever* – I wanna make a movie, so let's star in it together'. Then, in desperation, the director implores 'don't make a move!' as the strings shudder to a halt, and creeping on with the 'til I say *action*'.

'Here comes the hardcore live', he promises, full with antici-pation. Mark Webber's keening guitar and atonal strings accompany cried declarations of all the joys in wait; 'leave your make-up on, and I'll leave on the light', and increasingly sneered assurances – 'you can't be a spectator, oh no'; though soon she'd probably be wishing she was. The act itself is just a trudge, a repetitive, distorted crush, a matter of sheer, naked power, sex as victory with all of the earlier class-war righteousness very, very far away – all those are just excuses. 'This is *me* on top of *you*', and in a moment where amateur porn seems to be a means of really fulfilling other, less carnal dreams, or rather cementing them; not only pop star, celebrity, but also porn star, fulfilling the last possible fantasy – 'and I can't believe that it took me this long'. After that, post-coitally, it's just misery. The obsessed over real, the really making it, really doing it, is impossibly bleak. At first, as an unbearable tangle of strings slashes above, he's still telling himself a story about the value of what he's just done; 'this is the eye of the storm...it's what men in stained raincoats pay for, but in here, it's *pure*' – 'yeah', he derisively snorts, suddenly aware that 'purity' and the 'real' are just another performance, and an increasingly unconvincing one at that. What else is left? 'That goes in there, and that goes in there – and then it's over'. By the end, it sounds like a suicide note. 'The end of the line'. The orchestra melts away, passes out of tune, end. It's the moment in an amateur porn clip where the man forces the woman to look at the camera, where the fourth wall is breached as an act of realism, an alienation effect that Brecht could never have envisaged - that chilling, dead-eyed look into the lens.

'This is Hardcore' is about porn, of course, but it's also about the eventual telos of treating your life as a mediated thing, both in the sense that Jarvis Cocker clearly did, as a heavily plotted advance towards fame, power, or sexual success ('imagining a blue plaque') and in the sense of having lived your entire life exposed to simulacra, to, in Baudrillard's terms, reproductions without an original. It's not merely a matter of 'like in the movies', by any means, but something more fundamental, Christopher Isherwood's gleeful insistence that in California we have decided to live in our films, and we like it very much thank you, expanded worldwide. Pornography is the supreme example of this, and is hence in many ways the ultimate neoliberal art form – it's no coincidence that not only the United States, but also those post-Communist nations who have been most comprehensively evacuated of any non-monetary ethics or any remaining vestiges of solidarity – Russia, Ukraine, Hungary - have gigantic, lucrative and hyper-exploitative hardcore industries partly replacing the old world of heavy industry. And like the various neoliberal art forms anatomised in Mark Fisher's *Capitalist Realism*, the bizarrely critically unimpeachable gangsta principal among them, hardcore is all about the real, stripped of emotion, stripped of all but exchange value. Look, you can really see it going in; look, he's really coming. That goes in there, and that goes in there. Yet increasingly, one of the consequences of broadband and the accessibility of reproductive technologies is that 'This is Hardcore's scenario is now extremely common, thousands upon thousands of self-made films filling the archives of Youporn, Redtube, the tellingly-named Yuvutu. We are all pornographers now, and 'This is Hardcore' no longer sounds like one man using power and money to follow his own very particular perversions, but more like a deeply astute prophecy of a process of anticipation, copulation, depression and MPEG dissemination that has been repeated and repeated in countless millions of bedrooms over the last ten years.

As with the protagonists of *Ghost World*, Pulp's work always hinged on people living as if they were in a film, and something curdles by the time of 'Hardcore', when it entails making one. This is that ethos taken to its logical conclusion. The difference between the cinematic, obsessively detailed studies of everyday life in Pulp circa 1990-4 and this nihilistic final act, is in the difference between first taking the mundane in terms of surroundings, persons, places, and attempting to make it inter-esting via some kind of mediated revisioning, by imagining there's a film and you're the star – and, second in bitter contrast but as its telos nonetheless, taking the supremely mundane act of copulation and treating it as if it is some eternal truth. This is what makes the scenario so appalling. There's no Pink Gloves or Acrylics, no details. We learn nothing about his co-star (bar that 'leave your make-up on' - she could be a prostitute, someone he's just met or his wife, we are left with absolutely no idea). There's just the act and the camera - 'and that goes in there, and that goes in there, and that goes in there'. It's that minimalism which helps make it such an enduringly chilling record.

The video, rather adroitly, completely ignores the song's

narrative, for obvious reasons. Instead, director Doug Nichol creates an ambitious, utterly convincing analogue to the song's opulent, bleak, freeze-dried and inhuman world via an extraordinary essay in cinematic cliché; but it proved to be equally unscreenable, no more a viable pop video than a literal recounting of the song's story. It opens with two parodically American-looking, square-jawed men rehearsing dialogue, and then cuts to Candida Doyle, the star for once, standing for a screenshot and, after the Brechtian clapperboard, sat playing a grand piano in Hitchcockian style, dressed as one of the Leytonstone pervert's femmes fatales in a scarlet dress and a fetishistic, oversized green ring. The style throughout is an imaginary 1950s, opulent and psychotic, where all the characters have forgotten their lines but continue nonetheless, an amalgam of Hitchcock's most saturated, obsessive works – *Vertigo*, most of all – with the extreme unnaturalism of Douglas Sirk; American actors with striking physiognomy dominate, with the ungainly Englishmen and woman as the seedy, ill-fitting villains, the Peter Cushings of the piece. We first see the singer tied up in a private detective's office, singing through the rope around his mouth; buxom nurses filch jewellery from their dying patients as the life fades out of them; members of the group share cars with filmstars driving superimposed across googie landscapes; a series of crises take place in painstakingly furnished, alienatingly colour-coded rooms – a heart attack at a dinner party, a woman in lingerie dancing with herself; Jarvis Cocker dips his finger in a bloody mess on a pillow, as a dead woman in a basque lies beside him; clapperboards, jump cuts and strips of black are interspersed throughout, and the kind of structuralist interventions once used to charm now used to unnerve.

More than anything else, the 'This is Hardcore' video resembles the refracted 1950s-via-2000s California of Lynch's *Mulholland Drive* or *Inland Empire*, with a similar instability and inscrutability, squeezed into a tightly melodramatic space. Its main concession to the pop video genre comes when the singer finally takes centre stage, at the record's horrible core – the end of the line, the eye of the storm, what men in stained raincoats pay for – flanked by burlesque dancers. He begins prostate on the floor, then rises to stumble and shake through a leering mouthing of the lyrics, looking ill and joyless, framed by and falling through the dancers' feathers. It's still a performance, of course it is – but a performance that suddenly returns Pulp to the real outsiderdom of freaks, that aims in every gesture and tic to disturb. I don't recall it ever being broadcast on any of the major British pop TV shows, reaching neither *Top of the Pops* nor the second-rank world of *The O-Zone, CD:UK* or the shudder-at-the-memory Britpop magazine show *Jo Whiley*. Maybe hoping they could get it instead into late night Channel 4 or the cinemas, both this and the excellent video to 'Help the Aged' were squeezed into a half-hour *Do You Remember The First Time* style documentary, again by Martin Wallace and Jarvis Cocker, where the cast and crew or the odd celeb are asked about their various experiences of 'hardcore'; but it's all fairly prosaic after the hall of mirrors of the original six minutes.

A horror soundtrack from a stagnant water bed

After this extraordinary, and no doubt for their record company, entirely disastrous achievement, where next? The album, also titled *This is Hardcore*, seemed from the sleeve, the often mortified music press reaction, and the general commercial failure, to be carrying on the ruthless confessional project of the single. It wasn't, far from it – but the packaging certainly convinced many that it was. 'Directed' by Peter Saville, it was the finest sleeve that the City of Manchester's current Creative Director had produced since his mid-1980s work for New Order; indeed, it evokes the sort of thing that no doubt goes on in the Beetham Tower every night. *This is Hardcore* takes place in an ultra-modern and opulent hotel – specifically, that JG Ballard favourite, the London Hilton, whose cantilevered concrete balconies reminded Traven of the gill-slits of the dead actress, Elizabeth Taylor. If there's a Ballard comparison to be made here, it's to the haute bourgeois psychoses of *Super-Cannes* and – an apposite title here – *Cocaine Nights*, to that chilly world of hotels and airports, business travellers and prostitutes, random killings and the sex appeal of the inorganic. On the cover, a naked woman lies on a plush, red bedstead, with a blank look in her eyes either of despair or of death, her blonde hair tumbling over the sheets, her breasts pressing upon them. As a pointer to the effect this had on some of Pulp's fanbase, I recall my mother looking at it in disgust, shocked that a group she'd considered eminently right-on were creating imagery as unnerving and pornographic as this. On the back, a view of distant lights through strip windows; inside, a series of scenes 'directed by John Currin and Peter Saville', entailing photographs by Horst Diekgerdes worked into paintings by Currin, which are made yet more estranging through an alienating, pixellating device. Group members stand as the shifty voyeurs in the background of various pornographic acts; Mark Webber looks wide-eyed while two women undress each other, Steve Mackey looks disconsolate while a half-naked woman lies on the hotel floor, again conceivably either suicidal or already dead; and in the centre pages, Jarvis Cocker and some unnamed, tanned and cufflinked lothario prop up the bar, with the singer looking dishevelled, wasted and screw-eyed, as if caught in the act of surveying the bar's clientèle for prey. It's a chilling and scrupulously well-chosen analogue to 'This is Hardcore' – but not so much to *This is Hardcore*.

The album begins with 'The Fear', which is something between parodic nervous breakdown and the post-facto depiction of one. It begins, over horrorcore strings and guitars, with a series of lines proclaiming the new sound, the group's new aesthetic, as if to pre-empt the reviews, constantly looking over its shoulder. 'Our music from a bachelor's den...the sound of loneliness, turned up to ten...the sound of someone losing the plot...making out that they're ok when they're not'. The latter clause describes the album best of all, as it will, after 'The Fear's stark statement of intent, renege upon these various promises. It's an unnervingly eloquent depiction of depression, on the longing for 'some kind of life with the edges taken off' in no way lessened by its theatricality; and there's a few jibes, too at the imperative to write Indie Anthems – the chorus is as sweeping and catchy as anything on *Different Class*, but constantly upends any temptation the audience might have to sing along; in fact, that impulse is specifically mocked, around the time that enormous communal pub singalongs like Oasis-at-Knebworth were considered to be what all self-respecting acts ought to be aiming for. 'The Fear' ends with a series of guttural noises, the sound of malfunctioning machinery; and then, we're in something altogether more hushed.

If 'The Fear', is version one of the Britpop exit strategy – create something unnervingly adult, unfriendly, depressive and mocking of the possibilities of mass communication – then 'Dishes' is version two, better employed on the next album, the winded, self-baring ballad, pleading normality and begging for forgiveness. It's one of Jarvis Cocker's worst lyrics wrapped up in one Pulp's most gorgeous arrangements. Over an elegant arrangement of keyboards and chimes, so haunting and dreamy that it was used by Chris Morris as between-story material for his contemporary radio drama *Blue Jam* (whose slithering, prurient menace was close to *Hardcore*'s more extreme moments), are some of the most frightful self-abnegating rock hero clichés, an atrocious apologia, boasting the unironic plaint 'I am not Jesus, though I have the same initials...I am the man, who stays home and does the dishes...oh I am just a man, and I'm doing what I can to help you'; the hushed warmth of the delivery is such that you have to (with the song switched off, of course) read the lyrics to realise how bad it actually is. It suggests that its lyricist came across as far more arrogant the less cocky and boastful his words were. And as with most of the rest of escape strategy type 2, it disdains the position of overambitious public spokesman in favour of the previously mortifying domesticity. 'Party Hard' offers some reasons why that might be, in a rather-you-than-me-mate communique from the Groucho heart of mid-90s hedonism, where the previously smart manage to lobotomise themselves through coke, booze and of course the most venal of couplings; in lines like 'this man is dangerous...he just shed his load on your best party frock' you picture Alex James or Damien Hirst just out of shot. Musically, it's one of *Hardcore*'s more daring moments (this at a time when Mark Webber was citing La Monte Young and Steve Mackey hailing Aaliyah). Critics reaching for comparisons found its cretinised motorik charge to be a bit like Berlin-era Bowie, but it's closer to the Cold War Walker Brothers of 1978's *Nite Flights*: streamlined, compulsive, driven by lopsided, laconic crooned harmonies.

The obverse to its vacant, compulsive glide is 'A Little Soul', both *This is Hardcore*'s most conservative moment and its loveliest, a direct confrontation, 13 years after 'Little Girl (with Blue Eyes)' of the other party in the broken home, the philandering father; whom our protagonist desperately worries about becoming. Conveyed through a Philly Soul arrangement of strings and acoustics is a lyric, inspired by finally meeting his absent father, as brave as the earlier talk of porn and death. The macho chat up lines now sound horrible, misogynistic - 'I used to practice every night on my wife' – the father/Jarvis speaking to the son/Jarvis is filled with shame, both political and personal. Throughout, the first-person narrator keeps stressing his hope for 'soul', for a moment of sincerity, and as the song fades out, it's not clear he's capable of it; but the nihilism is gone for the moment, the defeat consoled through laughter in the dark. The latter two songs were *Hardcore*'s singles-off-the-album, both excellent, melodic, surprise-filled pop records with witty, imaginative videos that conclusively failed to lure back those who had been scared off.

Aside from these scattered moments of greatness, *This is Hardcore*'s failures are manifold. What's left centres around 'Seductive Barry', a lengthy, straight porn soundtrack like 'This is Hardcore' without the complexities and consistency, its lyric of unironic let's-get-it-on clichés appearing at first as an unconvincing surrender to carnal urges, without detail or much wit, its pleas seemingly directed at another 'star': 'and how many of us have touched themselves while looking at pictures of you? How many others could handle it, if all their dreams came true?' Its dragging, clotted atmospheres start with a heartbeat-pulse accompanied by vocoders and panting backing singers, before lurching into what at first seems to be a liberating consummation, which by the record's end sounds like a return to the sound of someone losing the plot. The song's original, far better title, 'Love Scenes', is a pointer that this isn't a real release, but a replay of an act heard earlier on the album. And if you hadn't heard This is Hardcore', 'Seductive Barry' would be a murkily compelling thing, but as you have already done so three tracks before, it's an overlong footnote. It sounded far better played live, as at their fractious, noisy return to Glastonbury in 1998, where a group led by a wired Jarvis in safari suit played *Hardcore*'s songs with a directness and violence too often smothered in Chris Thomas' suffocating, pro-tooled overproduction.

Not that some of those songs weren't unsalvageable anyway – the tossed-off 'I'm sorry I'm so bad' homily of 'TV Movie', barely worthy of appearing as a B-side, or the album's truly dreadful last third, a series of ever more pompous rock epics worthy of the late, please-split-up-now Manic Street Preachers. There's 'Sylvia', a cringeworthy power ballad boasting no less than two guitar solos, swamping a sometimes touching lyric, a protracted (and perhaps welcome) apology to a wronged, used and discarded woman, collapsing into a Noel Gallagher chorus – 'keep believing, and do what you do'. If aided by old Korgs and violins, something could have been made out of this, but it would always have been a salvage operation. 'Glory Days' is, as we shall soon see, the replacement for a far, far better song, lyrically a composite of great lines that never had anything coherent form around them, played in a galumphing manner clearly praying for another 'Common People'; 'I'm a Man', lyrically a tart anti-Lad statement, does the same with 'Mis-Shapes' but ends up sounding more like Meatloaf; and the closing 'The Day After the Revolution' is truly a group making out that they're ok when they're not, a failed attempt at catharsis. It imagines the great transformation, the new world's fervent creation, and you want to believe it as much as the lyricist clearly does; it ends with a series of curses upon the 1990s, upon Britpop's televised pseudo-revolution, upon guilt, cowardice, apoliticism, and, in the last line, irony. It doesn't work, the anthemic chorusing sounding forced, but it's a noble effort at creating some kind of closure. It concludes with a gorgeous, glistening ten minute synth drone – that La Monte Young influence in its only noticeable effect – and an unearthly, intoned 'goodbye'.

Around this time, Half Man Half Biscuit recorded a satirical jingle which could have been aimed at Pulp in 1998. The chorus went 'hey there, moody chops – you've only got yourself to blame; hey there, moody chops – you've gone and got national acclaim'. In places, it's hard to avoid disappointment, even retro-spectively, that *This is Hardcore* settled for being that most late-90s of things, the post-Britpop, New Labour-disappointment and coke-withdrawal comedown album, joining the genre with Blur's shambling, schmindie *Blur* and Elastica's eerie, smacked-out *The Menace*. To give them their due, it's to Oasis' enduring credit that they never insulted their listeners by presuming to inflict upon them an album on the perils of fame and fortune. Except Pulp, with their lyrical scruples, their refusal (lapsing sometimes here) to fall into cliché, were unable just to reproduce their erstwhile subject matter; in one interview, their singer commented that to stick with Sheffield vignettes, to murmur saucily 'I fingered her at t'busstop – alright' would have been insulting to those actually living that life. There were other things to sing about, though, than the hideous tricks on the brain caused by national acclaim.

You must be a socialist, cause you're always out on the piss

This is Hardcore is more than that of course, a lot more – but what makes it especially frustrating is that they had recorded the songs for a far more consistent record, for something which didn't hold back, which didn't step away from the brink half-way through in order to offer a succession of increasingly unconvincing reassurances. The outtakes and b-sides of *This is Hardcore*, some released at the time, others waiting until re-release in 2008, when pieced together with half of the original album, could have resulted in an exponentially more powerful record – the masterpiece that Pulp never actually managed to record, although *His 'N' Hers* and *Different Class* both came close. The b-sides of 'This is Hardcore' itself gave an indication of this at the time. It's odd, listening to them now, that they managed to lose their nerve over this in particular, especially given that releasing that song as a single was already an act of unrecuperable commercial suicide. What makes most of them so effective is a particularly unpleasant, but musically and textually highly effective combination of unleavened self-loathing and sonic experiment.

'Ladies' Man', for instance, is the sort of music you can imagine being listened to in the sleeve art's Hilton, a strikingly original piece of clipped, freezedried dub techno with a series of sexual boasts (or threats?) subsiding into shame and desperation, all sung through a vocoder in order to sound appropriately blank and evacuated, though the vowels and details ('stop looking like some housewife') show through. A similar track eventually released a decade later, 'My Erection', reused the synths/vocoder/swagger/self-loathing combination, but sounded yet more desperate, more propulsive. Both of them together could have satisfyingly replaced the aural procrastination of 'Seductive Barry'. And in place of 'TV Movie's embarrassing homily (plus whistling!) could have been 'Like A Friend', a sharp, disjointed account of betrayal which eventually ended up on the soundtrack to a remake of *Great Expectations*.

Meanwhile, the soul-baring of 'Dishes' might have been instructively contrasted with 'The Professional', released on the b-side of 'Hardcore', a sleaze-ridden, sample-driven strut where Jarvis Cocker takes himself most firmly to task for his various sins, to hilarious, if deeply uncomfortable effect. 'I know that you think I've lost it baby...I know you think that my star is fading...you don't fit those clothes anymore, why don't you take them back to the charity store...while you're there why not hand yourself in'; and then opting to go for the listener as well, into the bargain, promising them 'I'm only trying to give you what you've come to expect, just another song about single mothers and sex'. It at least manages to put across the Lacanian message of 'don't give me what I want, because that's not it' better than all that talk of just being an ordinary guy doing the washing up; the overall effect is akin to the episode of *Hancock's Half Hour* where Hancock finds out that he's been writing violently abusive poison pen letters to himself in his sleep. The careering glam of 'We are the Boyz', another song trickling out eventually onto a soundtrack (*Velvet Goldmine*, this time), put across the same men-are-scum line as 'I'm a Man' with vastly more aplomb and considerably less clutter.

Meanwhile, as portraits of women go, the stoically suffering female of 'Sylvia' ('her beauty was her only crime', etc) pales in comparison with the monstrous, charismatic protagonist of 'It's A Dirty World', the most finely, precisely drawn female character in a Cocker lyric since 1994. Inexplicably, this outrageously successful song, already given the full, claustrophobic, *grand guignol* Chris Thomas treatment, was held off *This is Hardcore* at the last minute. Alongside 'This is Hardcore' itself and another un-included song we will come to presently, it's the most lyrically striking thing recorded for it. Its nameless heroine, we are told, 'trained to be a dancer' ('she had a proper job by day') and is overpoweringly exciting - every bit as malevolent as the narrator, who has finally met his equal. A seething, lust-crazed vocal appraises someone who is, most likely from some of the lines, a stripper - 'the guys at the front have seen your act a million times and they all come back for more...you're making them feel so useless and dumb, 'cause they've seen it all and they *still can't come'*; the lust reaches combustible levels, as she dances 'until the place goes up in flames, then you lie down, in the charred remains – and that's where I come in, with my second-hand excuse for technique, yeah...' He's no real match for her of course, but is struck by some sort of tortured relief on finally, ineptly having her, on having found someone who actually compares to him. 'All I needed was a partner...and I'm so glad I found you', he groans over the churning, lurching beat. It's a fabulous record, and so much more *likely* than the album's apologies and fudges.

The most unforgivable absence of a song recorded for *This is Hardcore* from the album is 'Cocaine Socialism', a song which morphed into the considerably less remarkable 'Glory Days', something for which Cocker later confessed a regretful culpability; it ended up instead as the B-Side to 'A Little Soul'. Its subject matter, so undisguised that the libel laws were quite possibly the motivation for it being rewritten rather than mere cowardice, is a request by the New Labour government, after assuming power, to join one of its Cool Brittania receptions, where they could drink along with Alastair Campbell, Noel Gallagher, Alan McGee, Ken Follett et al. It's hardly undisguised. Over a transparent parody of the beatless, shimmering intro to

'Common People', an incredulous voice says 'I thought you were joking when you said 'I want to see you, to discuss your contribution to the future of our nation's heart and soul...Six o'clock our place, Whitehall''. The anecdote is wickedly, depressingly believable:

> I just want to tell you, that I love all of your albums...could you sign this for my daughter – she's in hospital, her name is...Miriam. Now I'll get down to the gist. Do you want a line of this, are you a – sniff – Socialist.

The 'Common People' parody builds momentum, with all manner of weirdness in the mix, from a derisive brass section to scrawled, feedbacking guitars and burbling synths. There are few better encapsulations of New Labour than what follows - 'just one hit and I feel great, and I support the welfare state...well you sing about common people, and the mistakes and the misfits, well can you *bring them to my party*, and *get them all to sniff this*'. They think they're *funny*, you see. 'Cocaine Socialism's viciousness was partly inspired by some of the first acts of the New Labour government – an immediate, and now-familiar attack on the weak, through the abolition of universal, free higher education, along with cuts to Lone Parent and Incapacity Benefit, neither of which were going to be taken lightly by someone who had spent almost the entirety of the 1980s on benefits of one sort or another. The sheer, insulting arrogance of presuming to speak for the oppressed while subscribing completely to the Thatcherite hierarchy of winners and losers was never better expressed. In this derisive, wonderful record, you can just smell the coked-up parties full of formerly principled government apparatchiks. 'We've waited such a long time, for the chance to help our own kind, so please come on and toe the party line...you owe it to yourself, you don't need anybody else – and we promise we won't tell – no, we won't *tell*!'

Most encouragingly, the malevolent, bleary, cynical Jarvis of 'Hardcore' is woken up from his slough of despond through a sudden rediscovery of the eloquent rage that ran through 'Common People' and 'I Spy'. It's 1998's only audible example of Jarvis-as-spokesman - but in the most unexpected and welcome fashion, at the point where some were still kidding themselves that New Labour offered much more than caring, sharing Thatcherism – it put into brutally effective words what many were thinking but unable to express, like the best political writing. It was, and is, extremely timely. Some of its justified anger would spill over into the best of what comes after.

Happy Endings

ANGEL: *My Lord, I hope this will not establish a precedent.*
DR REEVES: *I object! The rights of the common man -*
ABRAHAM: *The uncommon man -*
DR REEVES: *- the uncommon man, must always be respected.*
Powell & Pressburger, *A Matter of Life and Death* (1945)

How come no-one wants to know what I saw?

After *This is Hardcore,* there was another long hiatus – although this time, rather than an unnerving silence, it was filled by some encouragingly off-kilter side projects, all of them auguring for a much less bombastic and airless record on their return. There were some dabblings with television, much unlike the light entertainment dystopia catalogued in *TV Madness* – a Channel 4 series on outsider art, where Jarvis Cocker journeyed to various locations where ordinary, non-professional folk had created extraordinary artistic objects, the obsessively detailed, copiously decorated likes of the Facteur Cheval's Palais Ideal or the salvage art of the Watts Towers - estrangements of the everyday whose kinship with Pulp's work was easy to see. It was an enormously entertaining series, managing to avoid the creepy fetish for mental illness that is so often attendant on discussions of outsider art. There was a return to *Top of the Pops* with The All Seeing I, a South Yorks-themed concept group centred around one-half of erstwhile Sheffield techno gods Sweet Exorcist. Jarvis Cocker wrote the words to around half of the songs on their album *Pickled Eggs and Sherbet,* and they were the best pop singles he'd written since 1995, with the duties on singing them offered to his Sheffield forbears. The glorious, tragicomic 'Walk Like A Panther' was given to easy listening titan Tony Christie, whose dignity-on-verge-of-collapse tenor was perfect for a tale of miserable decline and replacement that might well have been about someone else entirely – 'Marie has run off with a man half my age...a halfwit in a leotard stands on my stage'. For the TV appearances, Jarvis sang it himself. Meanwhile 'First Man In Space' was given to Phil Oakey, recounting in that perversely expressive monotone the complete lack of interest those on his street had in his experiences outside of planet earth. On being asked for a sample lyric from the new Pulp record, the singer offered 'the juice of thy cunny is like a fine wine'. It all suggested it was going to be very good.

Even more so, when the songs they'd recorded for it first started to come out. To what might be expected to be a hostile, blokey audience at their only concert at the time, Reading Festival in 2000, the new songs – and the drastically re-arranged old ones – sounded curiously grown-up, loose, pointed, unflashy. Yet the just-a-tad 'Mis-Shapes-like 'Weeds', 'The Night Minnie Timperley Died' and 'Sunrise's entirely unexpected blast of space-rock, sounded as if Pulp hadn't entirely given up on the enduringly, dispiritingly popular verse/big chorus Anthemic genre. In the same year, the first fruits of the new album on record came out on yet another soundtrack that didn't deserve it, this time to Reeves & Mortimer's remake of *Randall and Hopkirk (Deceased)*. 'My Body May Die' was a collaboration with 1970s scat-singing troupe The Swingle Singers, or rather a beyond the grave dialogue between them and Pulp's singer, a complex and rewarding puzzle, a series of pledges of undying love with the singers sounding like a host of variety show spectres, while Pulp themselves create a piece full with chromatic, beatless subtleties. They didn't seem to be planning a big comeback, had no apparent interest in reclaiming their stage from those who were filling it, a mix of plodding, post-Britpop Anthem-peddlers like Coldplay and Snow Patrol or sprightly, derivative youngsters like The Strokes and their ilk. It suggested Pulp were going to head off into their own world quite happily.

For those who had fond memories of Pulp's previous rejection of these strictures, the monologues, soundscapes and epics that used to fill their albums, the main encouragement was a Peel Session in August 2001, where the stand out wasn't one of the new songs, but 'Duck Diving', a monologue read out from a short story called 'Return to Air' by Phillipa Pearce, which had been filched from a BBC Schools textbook, though at the time it was easy to assume the person reading it had written it himself. It's built around various samples, a string loop, birdsong and woodwinds, with the only non-sampled sound some skittering drums and buzzing synths. The narrative had a similar innocent, everyday joy to 'David's Last Summer', the longing-filled nostalgic monologue that ended *His 'N' Hers*. The narrator, a young, overweight woman, tells a story about diving into a river to find 'water like thick brown-greeny lemonade' and dreams of 'opening a sweet shop, or walking on the moon'. She brings out from the river what she first thinks is a brick, which on surfacing turns out to be an empty tin box, with all the paint stripped off it, which then provides a home for her coin collection. On 'Duck Diving' the group sounded liberated, the absence of the overstuffed production of *This is Hardcore* and the incessant need for a Big Chorus making them sound fresher than they had in years.

You try to shape the world to what you want the world to be

The album which followed in autumn 2001 was originally self-titled as *Pulp*, thenand then renamed at the last minute *We Love Life*; interviews and features stressed a new-found love of the bucolic and a fair amount of post-9/11 bluster about finding perspective, the death of irony and all that. Most exciting of all, it had been produced by Scott Walker, whose work was an overwhelming presence on Pulp's earlier records, whether the sweeping, affectionate but prurient catalogues of details and domestic dramas of *Scott* 1-4 on *Intro* and *His 'N' Hers*, or the 'torture chamber music' of *Nite Flights* and *Tilt* on *This is Hardcore*. It was the second time the elusive singer had produced another artist - the other was German cabaret chanteuse Ute Lemper a couple of years earlier, and that recording, 'Scope J', was lengthy, verbose and occasionally brutally noisy. But on *We Love Life* there wouldn't be much trace of Walker's lyrical and musical shifts since 1978. None of the abstract poetics, industrial clangs and atonal songspiels you find throughout *Tilt*, even less of the monolithic, barbaric sound of *The Drift*, which Walker was recording at the time. Instead, in what the credits imply was a very hands-on production, with Walker handling string arrangements and playing guitar on several songs, there's a pretty, orchestral and warm sound, vastly preferable to the crunching banality which concluded *Hardcore*. Walker's co-producer and collaborator Peter Walsh had produced Simple Minds' *New Gold Dream*, and that wide-open sound was palpable here too. If Chris Thomas could have been accused of smothering to death a couple of excellent songs, then here Scott Walker managed to flatter a few that didn't deserve it. Nonetheless, *We Love Life* is Pulp's *Abbey Road*, an elegant, forgiving attempt to bow out gracefully, not quite the masterpiece some hailed it as, but still the happy ending they deserved.

The sleeve, meanwhile, abandons the coherent look, the tightly wound aesthetic, of earlier albums for a series of works from more-or-less famous artists, all tilted towards the promised organic joie de vivre, all of them credited in the opening 'Contents', illustrations by Rory Chrichton or John Glashan and borrowed works by Peter Doig and Mat Collishaw. On the back of the booklet, the group are packed into a battered camper van, and Steve Mackey holds up a sign reading 'Bye'. It makes abundantly clear, as did interviews around the time, that this would either be the last Pulp album or the last for a very long time, and hence the pressure is off, leaving as their epitaph something that is suddenly so much looser and less severe.

It sweeps in with 'Weeds', a neat extended metaphor whose evident aspirations towards becoming a post-Britpop anthem – more-or-less the record's only particularly commercial moment, not released as a single - is made far more interesting than that might sound, through some imaginative production touches, with strange droning guitars, almost medieval percussion by Alastair Molloy, and glorious strings seemingly drafted in from some mid-century Biblical epic. Its 'marching off into the distance' pace fits perfectly with the lyric, which is the first communique for some time to the by now grown-up Pulp People. The 'Weeds' are both the weak and the wretched of the earth – specifically, and very unusually in a country where 'asylum seeker' has become an insult, beginning with figures who have 'come in from the North Sea with our carriers on our knees, wound up in some holding camp, somewhere outside Leeds'. The weeds are the marginalised, growing 'in places you don't go'; and they too promise revenge, that sooner or later 'we're gonna cut you down in your prime'. As soon as it fades out, it develops into the next track, 'The Origin of the Species', where the Weeds' predicament is now soundtracked by a fabulous proliferation of organic squelches, Swingle Singers backing vocals, synth flourishes and dub basslines. For all the talk of the bucolic and the rural, it's evident that we're really in the *rus in urbe* – 'found flowering in wasteland' – and the landscape is one where the commons has long since been enclosed, where the extended metaphor takes in class once more (absent from *This is Hardcore*'s private world), through some hissed warnings at those who might 'bring your camera, take a photo of life on the margins...offer money in exchange for sex...then get a taxi home'. The Weeds may look weedy, may seem to be in retreat, but the appearance is entirely deceptive – in fact, they're always potentially insurgent, capable of great destruction, wiping out all those private, sculpted 'planted trees and shrubs'. 'Their story has always been the same: a source of wonder due to their ability to thrive on poor quality soil, offering very little nourishment. Drinking Nurishment. But weeds must be kept under strict control, or they will destroy everything in their path'. In fact, we're back in 'Common People' all of a sudden, without recalling that song's sound in the slightest: you are amazed that they exist, and they burn so bright, whilst you can only wonder why. More than that - the two parts of 'Weeds' are 'Mis-Shapes' without the townie vs indie parochialism or the pop conformism, a last statement of proud outsiderdom. Listening to it in 2001, it was as if they'd come home after their rejection, decamped from their uncomfortable sojourn in the charts and the Hilton, and started making music again for those they were writing for and about in 1994 – but changed utterly by the experience, sounding sadder and wiser.

'The Night Minnie Timperley Died' inhabits a similarly minutely-observed space, a prolonged apology to a woman, akin to 'Sylvia' without the clichés or guitar solos. It's a grim story, about a teenage girl who is killed after a party on the edge of a city, by an older man. It's curious, especially given the interminable slayings in the work of contemporaries like Nick Cave, that this is the only one of Pulp's many songs about women ending in a death. It's packed with detail, from her own wide-eyed and innocent perceptions, to the more mordant notes on the party itself ('football scarves, the girls drink halves, her brother's crying, 'cause he has lost his decks'), to the description of her eventual murderer ('he thought he was still dangerous – paunchy, but dangerous'); and it has just an ounce too much sentiment. Nonetheless, given the hello-birds-hello-trees-hello-sky ethos of the album, it's not an especially optimistic song about the things that can happen outside of the city, where nobody is around to see. The next venture into the bucolic is equally cheerless. 'The Trees' is another sample-based thing, this time with a loop taken from the soundtrack to the film *Otley*, its tremulous strings, whose similarity to Scott Walker's 'Montague Terrace (In Blue) might not be coincidental, give off a sense of dignity in defeat. Nature is fit only for a life nasty, brutal and short, pervaded by decomposition and death, best expressed in the delightful first line 'I took an air rifle, and shot a magpie to the ground...and it died, without a sound'. The vocal, too, is almost unbearably poignant, recounting 'the smell of leaf mould and the sweetness of decay'. It's a series of admissions of conclusive defeat, and for all its gorgeousness it's hilarious that anyone thought it would make a single – a video where some ballet dancers contort around the silhouettes of bare trees hardly helped. It contains within it the most heartbreaking minute or so in Pulp's corpus – underpinned by the already overpoweringly melancholy sample emerges a little keyboard solo, cheap, tinny and hopelessly, hopelessly lovely. The disappointments and compromises of middle age seldom sounds so pretty.

As a single, 'The Trees' was double-A with the album's closer, 'Sunrise', which was surely even more unlikely as a potential hit. On the album, it tries to escape the melancholia, the decay and loss that pervade the rest of the record, through some kind of overdriven blast-off. It's the only time Pulp sound remotely convincing as a rock band. It's preceded by the particularly sad 'Roadkill', a list of memories, impressions and regrets, without rancour, clinging to memory in the absence of its subject. It joins several bucolic ballads on the record, of varying quality. 'Bob Lind' is a story about forgiven failures, about a commonality of fuck-ups, played and sung with such warmth and enthusiasm that it doesn't seem to matter that it sounds like REM; 'I Love Life' is, like 'TV Movie' on *This is Hardcore*, one of those soul-baring songs which sound like they were a damn sight more cathartic for Jarvis Cocker to sing than for the listener to hear; and 'The Birds in Your Garden' is a fairly straightforward *It* retread, surely an exemplar of Jarvis Cocker becoming nostalgic about his own work – only the mild naughtiness of the lyrics puts it beyond the pale of something like 'My Lighthouse'. It prefigures the mildly outré classic pop ballads he'd write throughout the 2000s for the likes of Nancy Sinatra and Charlotte Gainsbourg, someone settling for being a slightly seedy Bacharach who doesn't quite have the melodic gifts, hard to square with the outrageously original talent of 'Sheffield:Sex City' or 'I Spy'. For almost the entirety of *We Love Life*, the trends the two Chris Thomas albums started have continued – everything is tightly structured, with less monologues, less of the stunning shifts between monologue and squeal. They're all songs, and occasionally quite prosaic songs, for all their elegance; as a songwriter, Jarvis Cocker sometimes tends towards a leaden melodic predictability, the sense that you always know when the chorus is about to come in; something which sounds alternately like a willing embrace of cliché, filling it with new content, or simple laziness. There's one last hurrah of the earlier, freer, Pulp on *We Love Life*, a summation of all their urbanist epics, retranslated to their new, picturesquely overgrown environment.

I knew I had entered a completely different world

The Wicker is an area just north of Sheffield City Centre, where New Brutalist monuments like the Police Station, the Law Courts and the marvellous Castle Market peter out, replaced with a landscape of Victorian dereliction – disused factories, warehouses, old commercial premises, traversed by the stone Wicker Arches, lately with various uninspired new blocks filling the gaps, brightly coloured tat given names like 'the iQuarter'. It's also here that Sheffield's rivers converge, and theits long since abandoned docks sit here, disconsolate and bizarre so many miles away from the coast. 'Wickerman' borrows its title, of course, from the film *The Wicker Man*, whose soundtrack was released by 'music, nostalgia and sex' label Trunk Records, with all the dialogue left in, a tale of a pagan utopia, capable of astounding feats of agricultural production and with an extremely relaxed approach to sex, in a community which has successfully insulated itself from the outside world. Its imaginary heathen folk songs are sampled in the lower reaches of the mix, one input among many in a sweeping monologue.

The illustration here is a photo by Tom Miller, where a lonely trickle of silty water flows through concrete, setting up a song which finds in Sheffield's deindustrialisation a haunting drama, following the rivers Sheaf and Don through factories, wastelands and sudden, unexpected moments of traumatic beauty, accompanied by spiralling acoustic guitars, the sounds of the river itself, and the heathen cooing of Summerisle, walking us through a space saturated with memory. It starts in the city centre, and you could, if so inclined, plan a walk based on the song. It's very precise, practically a gazeteer. 'Just above the station, before you reach the traffic island, a river runs through a concrete channel. I went there with you once...the river was dirty, and it smelt of industrialisation...' Aligned by the river are various spectres from the city's past, 'little mesters coughing their guts up...connecting white witches on the Moor, to Pre-Raphaelites down in Broomhall' (respectively, a derelict shopping street, a ring-road and a waste where a council estate used to be). The past is vivid in the present, as we're told with relish about the 'old Trebor factory that burnt down in the early 70s, leaving an antiquated sweet shop smell, and caverns of nougat and caramel' – a child's fantasy city, where the proximity of the places where things are actually made leads to strange dreams and visions of abundance - '*nougat!*'

A quiet but mounting momentum is kept up, as the river

starts taking us through what appear to be characters from earlier Pulp songs, beside the conduits and concrete channels; we find the 'pudgy 13 year-olds addicted to coffee whitener' from 'Catcliffe Shakedown', 'courting couples naked on northern upholstery' straight from *His 'N' Hers*, 'pensioners gathering dust like bowls of plastic tulips' who might have been imagined 'clacking their tongues' in the face of the orgies in 'Sheffield: Sex City'. Then the submerged river 'comes above ground at Forge Dam, the place where we first met.' The momentum stops, a swell of strings, and we're on a different journey, 'hoping to find a child's toy horse ride that played a ridiculously tragic tune', a café with formica-topped tables; the place where he first kissed the 'you' the song is addressed to, 'and a feeling like electricity flowed through my whole body', with 'the sound of that ridiculously heartbreaking child's ride outside'. The prosaic space is estranged and romanticised through the kind of specific, vivid detail that elsewhere was slipping from the writer's grasp, in favour of generalities.

At the other end, we follow the river under an old railway viaduct. 'I went there with you once; except you were someone else', and learn about a local custom to jump off into the river after the pub, and that this custom had died out when someone sunk into the mud, and drowned. Then, six minutes in, Jarvis finally starts singing, and an urgent, desperate song forms out of these scattered memories and vignettes, as we approach the edge of Sheffield itself, filled with fear and anticipation - 'if we go just another mile, we will surface surrounded by grass and trees...and a flyover that takes the cars to cities', but do we really want to leave it anyway, to escape the city altogether? 'What lies ahead, I really could not say...' In the wildly romantic conclusion, we learn of an unfilled plan, when our protagonist was living in 'a disused factory, just off the Wicker' to follow the river all the way along, 'wherever the river may take me...wherever it wants us to go'. A drone and the sound of its disinterested flow remains as he departs. 'Wickerman' is a wonderful, partly because so unexpected, return to the territory of their most unusual, most sweeping work, that spoken word Sheffield-of-the-mind, the urge to encompass a city, to tell its stories, to reveal the layers upon layers of history, memory and longing that suffuse its most seemingly unlovely spaces and conduits. More than everything else on *We Love Life*, it sounds like a conclusive farewell. It's such a magnificent achievement that it makes the turn to straight love-songwriting elsewhere all the more frustrating.

I heard an old girlfriend had turned to the church

The 'official' ending for Pulp, at least before their reformation – which we will come to presently – was a brilliant and instructive song entitled 'The Last Day Of The Miners' Strike', released as the obligatory new song on *Hits*, a contractual obligation Best Of released on their departure from Island Records, whose commercial failure was apparently a surprise, even after the public failed, not unexpectedly, to make Pulp pop stars again. It presented the straightforward picture of Pulp as makers of great pocket melodramas (bar the out-of-kilter extremism of 'This is Hardcore'), and hence is Pulp as most saw them. An accompanying DVD with the same title was far more full of their ventures into uncomfortable or experimental territory; but the contractual obligation song made a decent enough epitaph.

The events that had a traumatic effect on Sheffield in the mid-1980s, the protracted 'Civil War without guns' of the Strike, the mass unemployment that convulsed the city, the seeming defeat in the class war that led to the scenarios of personal revenge and political betrayal in an 'I Spy' or a 'Cocaine Socialism' are finally given a direct treatment. The song has the same march-like, Biblical cadences of 'Weeds', beginning with the feeling of power and solidarity, 'people marching, people shouting...the future's ours for the taking now, if we just stick together', a force advancing towards victory. Except it's followed by 'the sound of horses' hooves, people fighting for their lives' (in nearby Orgreave, no doubt) and a defeat so drastic and conclusive that the last day of the strike is 'the Magna Carta in this part of town'; the singer himself is buried in poverty, but the force that he'd ignored at the time is absent; 'there's no one underground to dig me out and set me free'. And after that, we know the story only too well, 'In 87, Socialism gave way to socialising'; the north puts its hands in the air and pretends it's rising, only to be fooled once again. It's a potted and pessimistic political history of the two decades in which Pulp existed, the mostly unspoken background to all their actions being belatedly revealed. 'Lay your burden down', it insists, kidding itself that all this can be escaped.

As for the group's own brief, dramatic failed attempt at conquest, their entryist venture into the pop charts, the final riposte to that is in the video to 'Bad Cover Version', the only single-from-the-album pulled from *We Love Life*, like the album itself largely ignored by the record buying public. The song itself is an elegiac and knowingly ridiculous farewell, a mordantly arrogant send-off to those who had spurned them, all kisses like saccharine and a concluding list of replacements and ersatz versions. The video, directed for the last time by Jarvis Cocker and Martin Wallace, is modelled on those atrocious post-*Live Aid* charity videos where a variety of celebs get a line each in the aid of some cause or other, only it's populated with lookalikes, *Stars In Their Eyes* Bowies, McCartneys, Bjorks and Bonos, all singing ensemble for the refrain at the end. It's very funny, but in 2002 it had other resonances. At around this time, beginning with pop stars, the reign of the likes of Louis Walsh and Simon Cowell had its *Gleichshaltung*, the final elimination of all opposition and the collection of all forces into the leviathan. *Top of the Pops* was cancelled, and hence the only music television that had its immediacy, that was spoken about the next morning at school or at work, was pop as reality TV.

This reality was one where the unexpected, fantastical, vivid and vehement things which Pulp had consistently found in the everyday were completely and conclusively sidelined. The main virtues were, first of all, a compelling 'story' (although with their decade and a half of failure before fame, Pulp certainly had that), and secondly, an ability to mimic the gestures and the melismatic acrobatics of more famous singers – which, taken together, created an all-pervasive culture of conformity in pop which made the likes of Oasis and Menswear look like paragons of originality by comparison. Rather than being changed or upended, the British pop charts after the 1990s had reached a pre-1960s level of conservatism which was previously inconceivable; and the 'alternative' world was hardly in better shape, with the album charts and the rump of the music press dominated by the grossly sentimental epic anthemic balladry of 'landfill indie'. The 'Bad Cover Version' video was horribly prescient, in imagining a pop landscape made up solely of impersonators, other people's gestures, and the death of the weirdo pop star as anything more than a heritage reminisce. That something so bitterly angry, so musically off-message as 'Common People' could have been an enormous hit as recently as six years ago seemed absurd. The lineage that Pulp inherited died with them.

They will kill again

That's where we should leave Pulp, flouncing off with the muttered aside 'you're trying to replace me, but it'll never work'. Throughout the 2000s, it's hardly as if the world felt unable to carry on without them. Jarvis Cocker was alive and well and living in Paris, writing mildly outré classic pop songs for Charlotte Gainsbourg and Nancy Sinatra, doing the odd guest vocal for the likes of Richard X. By some measure the finest moment in his time as songwriter-for-hire was writing 'Sliding

Through Life On Charm' for Marianne Faithfull's 2002 album *Kissin' Time*, a ghosted autobiography whose malevolence, arrogance and drama was far more worthy of his talents than winsome ballads for famous people's kids, a glorious, lofty sneer sung in Marianne's aristocratic croak – 'suburban shits who want some class, all queue up to kiss my arse'. Pulp themselves backed her, doing the best of their 'Common People' retreads on what must be one of their last recordings. The rest are the typical dabblings of the off-duty pop star, some very worthwhile, some not; an album with Jason Buckle in 2003 as Relaxed Muscle, a pseudonymous electroclash project whose act entailed facepaint, bodysuits, snarling synthesisers and double-entendre-filled lyrics; a great idea on paper and occasionally very funny, but mostly an example of how much less interesting the sex was without the class. Cocker also curated an oddly conservative Meltdown festival at London's ultra-Brutalist South Bank (pausing to complement the place's architecture – 'concrete is a very underrated building material'). It was full of reformed teenage favourites like The Stooges and Devo, but also full of free events such as a programme of avant-garde shorts in the basement, and Carl Orff performances in the Royal Festival Hall foyer. He did a bit of radio, and recorded some solo records.

These two are largely beyond the remit of this book, as this is a book about Pulp, not about its frontman, no matter how much they might seem to be synonymous. That said, their evident bitterness gave off the whiff of the exiled revolutionary leader, surveying with disdain the period of restoration. They're two different versions of the mid-life crisis, and both much better than that sounds. *Jarvis* was decidedly similar to *We Love Life* in tone, elegiac and beautifully produced (by Graham Sutton of Bark Psychosis) but marred by some dreadful cliché – after the atrocious, lumpen rock conservatism of the first three songs on it, anyone who remembered 'Inside Susan' or 'My Legendary Girlfriend' would have have been forgiven never listening to it again; soon after, it builds into a bleak and mordant record about privilege and boredom, and a very worthwhile one. 'I Will Kill Again' or 'Disney Time' were riven with disappointment, catalogues of domesticity where the urge to re-emerge and reclaim his kingdom was amusingly obvious; the list on the former, where our protagonist resolves to 'get in to classical music...look at naked girls from time to time...log off in the nighttime...drink a half-bottle of wine' is simmering with suppressed rage. This spilled out completely on the 7″ single 'Cunts Are Still Running The World', a well-aimed and vindictive blast at the cant of Make Poverty History, the latest instance of the Live Aid absolution-through-rock genre, where the delusions of ethical capitalism, that the powerful could be swayed through the efforts of Bono and Thom Yorke, are mercilessly mocked – with this, and 'Cocaine Socialism' a few years earlier, it's possible to imagine an entire album of Jarvis-does-politics being an eminently good idea. *Jarvis* came closer to this than most.

The follow-up, *Further Complications*, was met with a fair degree of partly justified disdain; the second version of the midlife crisis, a strikingly transparent, self-implicating record about divorce and grimly swaggering philandering as a way of forgetting about it. He'd previously described Relaxed Muscle as a way of parcelling off his Id into a side project, but here it took centre stage. The album was produced by Steve Albini, 'reducer' of choice for the noisy, soul-baring record, the result sounding muddy, plodding and miserable. On extensive re-listening, masochistic or otherwise, there was something to its dissolute, dishevelled misery that was, if not exactly charming, so relentlessly nasty, so full of dark and unpleasant humour – or rather, full of someone trying to push his natural inclination towards humour into the most unpleasant places – that there was something to be said for it. 'Angela' is a greasy, propulsive leer at a woman 'nearly 23...earning £4.50 an hour'; 'Homewrecker!'

and 'Fuckingsong' were self-explanatory; and 'I Never Said I Was Deep' was the peak/nadir, where the roving middle-aged cocksman insists 'I'm not looking for a relationship...just a willing receptacle'. 'Slush' and 'You're in My Eyes' were fabulous songs entirely devoid of all this unpleasantness, the first a groggy ballad whose miserable tone was for once empathetic, without the fuck-off tone of the rest of the record, the other a disco strut with little evidence of Albini's bludgeoning touch.

But it might not entirely be a coincidence that, rather than being followed by another solo album, *Further Complications* was succeeded by the announcement that Pulp would be reforming to play festivals – in fact, reforming to their 'classic' 1995 line-up, Russell Senior included, though with an insistence that there would be no new material, and the unsurprising admission that they were doing it to pay off their mortgages. It would be forgiven to anyone not to have a feeling of 'et tu, Brute'? When Pulp had their fifteen minutes in the mid-1990s, it was mostly unheard of for groups to reform, and when the surviving Beatles pieced together John Lennon's dotage demos in 1995 or when the Sex Pistols went on tour in 1996, they were met with a justified hail of derision. Since then, it's easier to list those groups who haven't reformed – of those who still have all their surviving members, it's only really The Smiths and The Stone Roses – from those that have, a declension from The Stooges to My Bloody Valentine to NWA to New Order (playing Joy Division songs) to PiL to The Gang of Four to the Slits to the Pop Group to Blur to Suede to Shed Seven. It's easier to list the bands who recorded something of note after reforming; Scritti Politti, a solo project in all but name, or Wire and the Human League, who recorded fine albums but who had never quite split up in the first place. And that's about it.

It's hard to resent the reformation *too* strongly – they'd only ever claimed to be on 'hiatus' after all (albeit a ten year one, by now). Given that Pulp's royalties were split six ways, and that on the last two records especially, their production might well have cost rather more than their consumption, they might genuinely need a few quid. But especially given how perfectly and adroitly they'd ended in 2002, it's a shame to find them joining the Britpop nostalgia circuit. The Pulp People website, the nearest thing to an official statement, is full of uncertainty as much as excitement, devoted entirely to a series of 'FAQs regarding the band Pulp's 2011 concert tour'. Most of them are somewhat pointed. 'Is this some kind of a joke? Is this nostalgia? Is this a miracle? Is this a collective mid-life crisis? Is this a chance to see the last truly important pop group this country produced? Is this the final straw?' and most pointedly of all, 'is this an opportunity to reappraise the past viewed through the prism of the present day?' One, 'is this just the kind of tonic the nation needs at the moment?' implies that this could so easily be the 90s pop nostalgia equivalent of the Royal Wedding, a big communal singalong through the bad times. It'd be tragic for Pulp to be reduced to this, more tragic even than being reduced to waving your arse at Michael Jackson.

If Pulp represent the last flourishing of a lineage, then it's likely that anything new and emergent would have another name, other components – perhaps by those who don't give a damn for them in the first place, who might reject them as well as the rest of the museum culture that pop music has so irretrievably become. Yet, looking at the political landscape of the 2010s in the UK – mass unemployment, a seemingly unending slump, an ever-widening north-south divide, a sneering, rapacious class war so far fought only on one side by people who clearly have no idea how most of the population live - and, most of all, the fraternising between the worlds of academia and working class youth on the student protests, it's hard to imagine the book is wholly closed. Pulp don't deserve to be slotted away with the rest of the tedious Brit canon. Their work reanimates the mundane cities we trudge through, speaks bitterly of the inequalities we ignore and tolerate, and is carried most of all on a refusal to forgive and forget the slights inflicted upon us. A refusal ever to 'get over it', an insistence on maintaining the resentments and grudges that will one day explode. Look out; they'll tear your insides out.

Acknowledgements

I'm obliged to those who read over and commented on the manuscript, whose suggestions I've often incorporated – so thanks Tariq Goddard, Richard King, Carl Neville and Ben Pritchard.

Thanks also to everyone who suggested names for this book when I appealed on the internet - even although I didn't use most of them for much more than subheadings, they were excellent, even the ones that were awful.

I am profoundly indebted to the proprietors of PulpWiki and acrylicafternoons.com.

Special thanks to Lydia Thompson for her cover and for inspiration, and to Lisa Cradduck, for her etchings and for getting it.

Finally, fulsome thanks to Agata Pyzik, whose suggestions, dissensions and argumentativeness enlivened the writing of this book, and from whom a couple of the best lines are pinched.

Fear not brothers and sisters, we shall prevail.

Warsaw, January 2011.

Contemporary culture has eliminated both the concept of the public and the figure of the intellectual. Former public spaces – both physical and cultural – are now either derelict or colonized by advertising. A cretinous anti-intellectualism presides, cheerled by expensively educated hacks in the pay of multinational corporations who reassure their bored readers that there is no need to rouse themselves from their interpassive stupor. The informal censorship internalized and propagated by the cultural workers of late capitalism generates a banal conformity that the propaganda chiefs of Stalinism could only ever have dreamt of imposing. Zer0 Books knows that another kind of discourse – intellectual without being academic, popular without being populist – is not only possible: it is already flourishing, in the regions beyond the striplit malls of so-called mass media and the neurotically bureaucratic halls of the academy. Zer0 is committed to the idea of publishing as a making public of the intellectual. It is convinced that in the unthinking, blandly consensual culture in which we live, critical and engaged theoretical reflection is more important than ever before.